From

RECEPTIONIST

to

BOSS

nicole Smartt

From

RECEPTIONIST

to

BOSS

Real-Life Advice for
Getting Ahead at Work

Nicole Smartt

Published by Advantage, Charleston, South Carolina.
Member of Advantage Media Group.

ADVANTAGE is a registered trademark and the Advantage colophon is a trademark of Advantage Media Group, Inc.

Printed in the United States of America.

ISBN: 978-1-59932-691-7
LCCN: 2016932264

Book design by George Stevens & Katie Biondo.

This publication is designed to provide accurate and authoritative information in regard to the subject matter covered. It is sold with the understanding that the publisher is not engaged in rendering legal, accounting, or other professional services. If legal advice or other expert assistance is required, the services of a competent professional person should be sought.

Advantage Media Group is proud to be a part of the Tree Neutral® program. Tree Neutral offsets the number of trees consumed in the production and printing of this book by taking proactive steps such as planting trees in direct proportion to the number of trees used to print books. To learn more about Tree Neutral, please visit **www.treeneutral.com.**

Advantage Media Group is a publisher of business, self-improvement, and professional development books and online learning. We help entrepreneurs, business leaders, and professionals share their Stories, Passion, and Knowledge to help others Learn & Grow. Do you have a manuscript or book idea that you would like us to consider for publishing? Please visit **advantagefamily.com** or call **1.866.775.1696.**

To my mom, the most inspirational woman in my life, for teaching me to set my goals high and never stop until I reach them. To my dad, for showing me how to work hard and that just being good at something is not enough. Thank you both for your constant love, support, and encouragement to be the woman I am today.

TABLE OF CONTENTS

INTRODUCTION

I may have been born Smartt (that's my last name), but I wasn't born lucky or rich. My parents were not wealthy or famous. As a family, we were comfortable. I took horseback-riding lessons every Saturday, and one year, my dad invested in my sports career by sending me to basketball camp. After horseback-riding lessons, I would go to work with my dad, helping him in the warehouse by cleaning or stocking items while he worked.

Like many other kids, I knew that attending a traditional university right out of high school was a pipe dream. My family couldn't afford the cost, and besides, I didn't have clear professional goals that would merit such an investment. Investing thousands of dollars when I didn't even know what I wanted to do just seemed foolish.

My First Step

So I started where millions of kids start: at the local mall. At age sixteen, I began working two jobs, one at a Claire's jewelry and accessories store and the other at Saks Boutique, which sold high-end purses. I certainly didn't see either as the beginning of a career path, but they were. I learned almost immediately the value of helping customers, being a good employee, doing what was expected, and most of all, of being loyal to the people who worked alongside me. So when my manager recruited me to go with her when she left Saks to manage a store on the other side of the mall, I said yes and became her assistant store manager.

1

I was eighteen. I had graduated from high school, but like most eighteen-year-olds, I didn't know what I wanted to do next. High school didn't exactly provide me with much of a calling—but Saks and Claire's did! I learned the basic rules of success: show up, work hard, be friendly, help others, and make every task count.

Not exactly a college education, but a start. Since I didn't know what I wanted to do with my life and I couldn't afford to invest four years in an expensive university without a clear goal, I did the next most logical thing: I began exploring new opportunities by taking classes at Santa Rosa Junior College (SRJC).

Life beyond the Mall

After I began taking classes at SRJC, I started looking for a professional life outside the mall. The SRJC Career Center helped place me in a part-time receptionist role at Remedy Staffing, a company that matches people with the employers who want to hire them. It was a step away from retail, meeting the immediate needs of young consumers and doing something more abstract and meaningful. Helping match people with jobs meant having the opportunity to play an important role in the lives of everyone I met. I was on the bottom rung of an industry devoted to helping people who wanted to help themselves.

The Power of a Mentor

I made an immediate connection with Cathy, the office manager, whose son was a schoolmate of mine. Cathy not only helped me get the job, she continued to be a mentor and advocate for me even after the company closed its branch in San Rafael, California. By the time that happened, I'd learned the business and was going above and beyond my role as receptionist, trying to help clients and colleagues however I could. When they asked Cathy to run a branch in Santa Rosa, she asked me to come along. Now, instead of following my boss across the mall to a better job, I was working in the real world, where the stakes were higher. Through this transition, I thrived and grew in confidence and capability. Cathy saw this transformation and took me away from the receptionist's desk by convincing the owners—and me—that I would be successful as a recruiter, a key job in the staffing business.

When Destiny Got in the Way

I discovered something else: a job was more than just a place to put in time for money. It was a way to grow, personally. As a recruiter, I did just that: I worked long hours voluntarily and kept striving to do my work better and improve processes as I went. By age twenty-one, I was asked if I wanted to buy the company.

I said no.

I felt I was too young to own a company, and I wasn't prepared to take on that risk. I've tried not to spend a ton of energy on regretting that decision.

Meanwhile, Remedy was sold to a larger company, Select Staffing, and when the new owners took over, I became a sales representative. I stayed for two more years and then left, planning to start my own company. It didn't happen quite that way. As fortune would have it, another staffing firm, Star Staffing, had been interested in hiring me since my days as a sales rep because I had made such an impact on my industry and community. When they approached me and asked if I wanted to become a sales representative, I told them I had no interest in doing sales—that I had a vision for what I saw as an employee-centric, fast-growing company that would dominate the market.

When they heard my interest in becoming an owner, they confided in me that the president of Star was in the process of exiting the industry. The timing was amazing. I initially joined the company in August 2009 as a regional sales manager. I had to prove myself with Star and show that I would fit the company's culture, add stability to the company during a time of transition, and bring significant revenue with me. I accomplished this in the first three months, and the negotiations started with the legal team. In October 2010, after proving my promised success, I became vice president and co-owner. I had become an owner by age twenty-five.

We make our own fortunes, despite our occasional reliance on timing and "luck." Star's management team recognized my potential, and as we discussed more deeply my ideas and vision, they became certain of my fit, and we joined forces. Luck happens to disciplined, hard-working people who are paying attention and who know their own limits (and when to push them).

What This Book Will Give You

What you are reading is the story of how I got to where I am today and the things that worked for me and made my success possible. Take advantage of my experiences. If you do, you will see that they will guide and inspire you to overcome the odds you face, help you become the extraordinary person you can be, and propel your career forward, in whatever job or industry that may be. The chapters in this book are a blueprint of how I went from receptionist to business owner in less than seven years and how you can too. Read it. Own it. Take action.

Smartt Steps

THE FIVE SMARTT RULES OF SUCCESS

1. Show up.

2. Work hard.

3. Be friendly.

4. Help others.

5. Make every task count.

Merriam-Webster *defines passion as*
"a strong feeling of enthusiasm or excitement for something
or about doing something."

STEP ONE

Get Excited about What You Do

I did not become a receptionist at Remedy Staffing because I was passionate about recruitment or job placement or about being a receptionist. It wasn't until later that I realized the larger importance of helping people find work and helping employers find good team members. At the time, I took the job because I needed one, and experience working in an office can't ever hurt. In my role, I was given a multitude of tasks, many of which were tedious and repetitive. I could have done the job without enthusiasm or excitement. But instead, I took every chance I could to ask for *more* work, even the tedious kind. I worked hard, and I was given more and more assignments.

Passion as a Prize

Because I had generated real enthusiasm for what I was doing, I didn't let all that work get me down. My heart was in it to win it, and I knew that what I was doing was making my manager's job a little easier and mine a little more valuable, just by being reliable and doing my best. So I continued to take on payroll tasks and then sales and recruiting tasks, and within a year, I moved from receptionist to recruiter. Success is not easy, but when you are enthusiastic about what you do, the stress, challenges, and bumps in the road are easier to overcome. Passion serves as a driver, the thing that sustains you when things get tough.

When I took the job as receptionist, I committed to being the best receptionist I could be. Find the good in your job. Maybe it's the simple fact you're not working weekends or the fact that you're making an impact on other people's lives, or maybe it's that your job is a stepping stone to a very prosperous career. Remember that and channel the positive. You create your own destiny.

Five Ways to Know You've Found Your Calling

There's a lot of talk in today's work world about finding your calling. Before you can fulfill your calling, you've got to identify what it is. But no matter which of the countless schools of thought you embrace, there doesn't seem to be much out there about how you can tell when you've found it. Here are five ways to know when you've arrived on the right road.

1. **Your ambition is alive and well.** If you find yourself voluntarily researching and learning new skills that support what you're working on and if you're networking on your off hours—work just comes up in social conversations and your excitement is infectious—then you're probably on the right track.

2. **You're content.** The feeling that there's something "better" out there for you—something you might enjoy doing more than what you're doing now—is gone. Yes, it's possible! There's a moment when the question of whether or not you're spending your energy doing the right thing,

regardless of the financial compensation, sort of stops mattering. You wake in the morning knowing that you're putting your effort to good use. This could also be a sign of burnout, which we will touch on in Step Four.

3. **You've found your people.** You'll realize you're increasingly surrounded by like-minded people. Your excitement, determination, and great ideas will feed others. A side note: if you feel as if you're far more deeply committed to what you're doing than those around you, you're probably partway there; you may have found your calling but not your people yet. Stick it out.

4. **Your work doesn't feel like work anymore.** This is true at least most of the time. You'll be glad to put on your proverbial work gloves and put your best efforts into it.

5. **You are aligned with your core values.** I saved this one for last because it may be the most important, but it can also be very difficult to identify. If your values aren't compromised, your ideas will flow freely. This is, in part, because you trust yourself, the group you're working with, and the goals for which you're striving.

If you're on the fence about whether or not you've found your calling, wait it out awhile. Give yourself as much time to think as you need, but don't jump ship just yet. It's a process, but keep faith. You'll get there.

Listen for a Calling

When I was a receptionist at Remedy Staffing, people would come in and tell me their stories, thinking that I was the recruiter and that I was going to be the one placing them. I had given them the paperwork, after all, and then they sat directly across from me, so it was a natural assumption. They would ask a lot of questions about the application, and I would answer them, and then they would start telling me about themselves. The people skills I demonstrated indicated I might make a good recruiter. I just had to pay attention to the signs.

The Man on the Bike

One day, a man rode his old bike to our office. That was an odd thing to do in Marin County, California, one of the most expensive places to live in the San Francisco Bay Area. He started doing his paperwork, and during that process, he confided that although he had held quite a few great jobs in the past, recent circumstances had resulted in his seeking refuge at a homeless shelter. We were able to get him back on track by connecting him to a job. The last time I checked, he was still there, and he had first come to our office in 2004. He was able to get his feet back under him, and I was excited that I'd helped him achieve that.

I was a receptionist, and I enjoyed talking to people and finding out their histories, talking to clients—the people looking to employ our applicants for specific jobs—to find out what they were looking for in a candidate, and then making that match. Helping people get in the door of these large companies was fulfilling. I was making an impact.

Although I was passionate about my work at Remedy, I still did not know it was my calling. Sometimes, you know what you want, and you're ahead of others in that journey. But oftentimes, you land in a position and only after that begin to understand your purpose. This is what happened to me. I enjoyed the challenges and positive outcomes and began to see this as a real career path. The same could happen for you. You never know where your current position will lead, so always perform at your best.

Find Your Passion through Your Strengths

When considering your strengths, make sure they're practical. Strengths aren't necessarily what you want to do or even things you like doing. They're what you are good at. When I first started out, my list of strengths didn't include staffing expertise. Instead, it included these qualities: creativity, competitiveness, and determination. I knew I also liked to be rewarded, so I needed to be in a position in which I was appreciated and valued because that gave me even more drive. What didn't make it on my list, until I discovered I was already doing it successfully, was that I happen to possess the kind of outgoing personality that makes a person good at sales and at speaking in a boardroom. And that was a surprise, since I was the kid who hated speaking in front of the class!

Taking on the sales role was a huge challenge for me, but I knew if I didn't try, I would regret it. Plus, when they asked me to move to sales, they promised that if I didn't like that position or didn't perform well, I could go back to recruiting. In my industry, and in most others, sales is, ultimately, about building relationships, and I had a strong track record of that, mostly through phone calls and e-mails, which are all varieties of *inside* sales. But since *outside* sales in that environment were conducted on a person-to-person basis, I was nervous. For the first year, walking into corporate offices and trying to speak to the hiring manager was nerve-wracking, but through practice and making my target (twenty-five calls a day!), I got better and better.

Fast-forward, and now I am running a company of forty employees, holding town-hall meetings where we all get together to discuss how we are doing, and presenting to CEOs, CFOs, and executive teams in boardrooms, pitching our services. Recently, I spoke in front of fifteen members of an executive and management team to pitch my company's services for a multimillion-dollar account.

My list of strengths has changed over the years and yours may change too. With practice, determination, follow-through, creativity, and staying true to your word you will discover hidden strengths you never knew you had—skills that will help propel you into a successful career.

Learn Something from Everyone

I quickly realized that if I was going to learn, I'd need to learn from the best. Nadine and Carl, the owners of Remedy Staffing, were those people. In my eyes, they were the epitome of success.

Carl and Nadine allowed me to see, firsthand, how they managed their business. If you have the opportunity to work with owners at any level, take it. The wealth of knowledge you will gain is priceless. Carl and Nadine were very hands-on in their business. As a husband-and-wife duo, Nadine handled client relations while Carl handled management and finances.

Find little things about your job that you really enjoy, and do them very, very well.

When you have two managers, you have to remember that while they may have similar goals, they don't necessarily have similar personalities. I got to know two different people, and I got to take what I wanted from each of them to become what I felt was the perfect fit for the business. I learned to look at everybody as a mentor. And why not? After all, you can learn from everybody. So ask questions, listen carefully, and discover passion for what you're doing. Your mind is a powerful tool. Find little things about your job that you really enjoy, and do them very, very well. Make sure you bring all of your skills to your work. You'll find you enjoy it because you're good at it.

Preparation Is Essential

As kids in school, we were always studying for tests and quizzes. That doesn't actually stop when we move to the business world. The more prepared you are, the more likely you are to succeed. Even as a receptionist, I came to every meeting with my notepad and pen and wrote down every single significant comment that was made. It may have been a bit much, but I was able to study that notepad and understand more about how meetings are run, the way the agenda flowed, and how people showed up to the meeting. When I had Cathy's (the office manager), Nadine's, or Carl's time, I came prepared with questions ready to go. I was efficient and to the point. It showed respect and leadership characteristics.

One of the things that really got people's attention back in my receptionist days wasn't just the eagerness of my note taking. It was that I became more useful to others when I used the information I had gathered, especially when analyzing situations and my role in them. The other thing that seemed to attract supportive attention was putting things in motion. Meetings are part of most jobs. People attend, talk a lot, and go back to their desks. I realized that what sets high achievers apart from all the others is what they do *after* the meeting. When you stay true to your word and can be counted on for accomplishing action items, people will take notice.

Make Yourself Matter

Be a person who shows up early, is prepared, asks questions, and leaves a meeting committed to accomplishing those action items. You'll be seen as a person who can be counted on. That's an A-player in my book.

Friday Night Meetings

After I became a recruiter, I started observing the times of the day when Nadine and Carl would come in. Carl would arrive first thing in the morning, and Nadine would arrive after lunch. They would stay late almost every day but particularly on Friday nights. Nadine would come into my office around ten 'til five on Friday evening to discuss day-to-day things. When she walked in, just before quitting time, I could have said I had to go, but I realized those end-of-day visits were great opportunities. It was during those after-five, one-on-one meetings that I learned the most about the business. My obvious interest gave me a chance to demonstrate how *truly* dedicated I was. When everyone else was leaving at the end of the workweek, I was in my glory and getting all the attention—and the approval—of my bosses.

Five Lessons I Will Never Forget

1. **Become a sponge.** Absorb as much information as you can.

2. **If you're going to fail, fail fast.** Learn from it, grow, and correct it. Don't let the same mistake happen again, and don't carry it with you once it's behind you.

3. **Hard work beats traditional education.** I don't mean to suggest that there's no point in a traditional education, but if you have little formal education, hard work will always pay off. Don't limit your options based on schooling alone; if you want something, fight for it.

4. **No job is too insignificant.** From the start of my career, I wanted to learn every set of skills I could. Even though I didn't always get paid for taking on tasks that fell outside my job description, I advanced more quickly as a result of my effort to learn.

5. **Never get too far away from customers.** This didn't resonate as much until I became a recruiter and really understood the power of the customer. Nadine was running a business, yet she always was involved with clients. Every week, she had a planned lunch with a top client.

Be the Best You Can

You think you're "just" a receptionist or an administrative assistant. You're not. *You're the best receptionist that company has ever seen.* Don't downplay the work you do. You are the face and voice of the company! Take your job seriously. We all start somewhere, and I wouldn't be where I am without that exceptional front-desk experience. Be it. Show it. Embrace it. You've taken the first step.

Smartt Steps

Exercise: Get to Know Your Strengths

1. Know your strengths. I personally like *StrengthsFinder 2.0,* a book by Tom Rath. It contains a twenty-minute assessment test and outlines your five greatest strengths. I like it because it reveals that what you may think are your strengths are actually not. It can be good to have a second set of eyes, so to speak, to help you understand your strengths from a new perspective. There are other strength assessments available for free on the web.

2. Preparation is key. Sit down and do a detailed self-analysis. Come to your review with a comprehensive understanding of how you see your performance, what roadblocks you have been encountering, and your steps to remove those roadblocks. Be prepared with solutions that show you care. That extra step will convince others that you are an essential team member.

3. Find meaning in what you do. By doing your best at whatever you do, you'll discover your passion. It's easier to find a perfect attitude than it is to find a perfect job. Once you embrace your passion, you can put it to work! Let your engagement and happiness show in all you do.

It's easier to find a perfect attitude than it is to find a perfect job.

EXERCISE: SPARK YOUR PASSION

1. List your common tasks.

2. Find at least one reason that makes each task important.

3. Visualize what your tasks mean. How many people do they impact? What would happen if nobody was doing these tasks?

4. List the strengths that make you the right person to do these tasks.

5. Envision how this new knowledge might help you feel more passionate about your work.

"Work like there is someone working twenty-four hours a day to take it all away from you."
M ARK C UBAN

S TEP T WO

Make the Most of Your Twenty-Four Hours

W hen I was in high school, I arranged my class schedule so I could get out as early as possible to work and save money. During my junior and senior years, I had long days. I got out of school at a quarter of twelve, and I'd work from one to five. I'd usually have basketball practice from half past five until half past six or seven in the evening. Then it was home to dinner, after which I'd start homework—unless there was a game, of course, and then I'd have to work out scheduling changes with my employers.

I learned early in life that time is precious, and that as long as you're on this planet, you have only twenty-four hours in a day. Ever notice how some people accomplish three times as much in a day as others? They maximize their time. Right now, think about the time you spend watching television, listening to gossip, and looking at other people's social media pages. These activities can add up and waste time you could be spending making yourself a better person. The secret is to choose wisely what you do and with whom you spend your time. It's about saying no, staying focused, and avoiding distraction.

19

The one-word secret to getting everything done? No. Say it every time you feel you're being distracted.

Distractions Are Everywhere

They multiply with growth and opportunity. There weren't as many distractions when I was a receptionist, for example, because the scope of my responsibilities was considerably smaller. And social media didn't exist then! But when I became a recruiter, distractions became more frequent the busier I got.

Avoid Time Bandits

Determining which tasks are time sucks and which aren't can be tough, but I have found *the single most disruptive time suck at work is incoming message pings.* For a single event—say, receiving an e-mail—you might get six pings. Turn off as many as is feasible, and you'll be in a better position to move your own strategic plans forward. While we're talking about pings and disruptions, when you're at work, be at work. Think about the five minutes you spend here and there, looking at your phone or checking a Facebook page or liking a comment. It all adds up and robs you of productive time.

Set Your Intentions

When you have a phone call or a meeting, set the expectations immediately and put a timeline on it. When I was a recruiter, I had an overload of candidates wanting to meet with me, clients expecting me to respond within minutes to an e-mail, and an endless string of callers who kept the phones constantly ringing. To maximize my time, I would remind myself of my intentions each time I took a call.

I would keep in the front of my mind the goal of the phone call for myself and the candidate or client. This saved a lot of time.

Schedule Everything in Your Calendar

Scheduling is essential for keeping you organized and focused on long-term goals while pursuing immediate opportunities. Every time I would commit to a meeting, it went into my calendar, including family and friend events. This helped me stay on top of what I was doing every day of the week. If you do the same, you'll find it helps to have easy access to all of your commitments, which, in turn, helps you prioritize and manage your time wisely.

Seven Simple Ways to Make Every Hour More Effective

We have all read books that tell us how important our time is, but most books don't explain in any detail how to take steps to manage time more effectively. Well, I will. I live by these techniques and share them with others whenever I have a chance. Adopt these techniques for yourself, and you'll find you are able to manage your time better so you can invest more of it in developing yourself, your business, and your leadership.

Not every tip will work for everyone, but choose the ones that resonate most with you and make a start.

1. **Start by organizing and simplifying.** Label files in a way that makes sense to you. *Keep important, frequently referenced documents in a folder.* The less time you spend searching for items, the more time you have to focus on important tasks. We all get inundated with work-related

details, but we need to remember that taking the time to organize now saves time in the future.

2. **Multitask with intention.** We live in a fast-paced world where people continuously take on more work than they can possibly accomplish. By multitasking, you can achieve a lot more. But let me be clear: *it is very important not to multitask to the point where you lose focus.* For example, if you are on the phone with a client, you probably shouldn't be typing an e-mail. The gym, however, is a great place to get a lot of work done. Jump on the elliptical machine and spend the hour working the lower half of your body while sending e-mails. You'll still get an incredible workout and you'll feel less stressed afterward, having accomplished both your fitness and work goals.

3. **Write your to-do list the night before.** A surprising number of very successful people share this habit. Knowing what your workload will look like the following day will help you rest more easily. You'll also be able to refer to it if you realize you've forgotten something overnight. Writing the to-do list means part of you will be thinking about the following day's activities, helping you feel more prepared to meet unique challenges or new situations.

4. **Read *Never Eat Alone* by Keith Ferrazzi.** This is one of the most inspirational and informative books I've ever read. Ferrazzi details, in entertaining anecdotal fashion, the best tactics for networking effectively, with generosity, and in a way that ensures everyone wins. Our lives, in business and

outside of business, are largely dictated by the health and strength of our connections.

5. **Set aside personal time.** When you're done at work, be done with work. An unbalanced life isn't healthy. Just as our bodies and minds need the rejuvenation of sleep, our "work muscles" need time to rest, recuperate, and ruminate on new information. Remember to commit as much time, effort, and love to your nonwork relationships as you put into your work relationships (including time with yourself).

6. **Turn off the TV.** Invest in yourself. Instead of submitting to the urge to tune out in front of the tube, read something. Whether you're reading something that will directly help you improve your performance, strategy, or outreach at work or you're reading a book strictly for pleasure, you'll be doing yourself a great service. Our minds need new information, and from varied sources, to continue growing.

7. **Listen to audio CDs while driving.** There is so much to learn—and so little time to learn it all. Audio books are readily available, both on CD and for download (try www.audible.com for a wide, high-quality selection). That long commute could work in your favor. Start your day with a motivational CD to get you pumped up for work, or listen to an industry-specific talk to gain insight and new tools. And don't forget the thousands of free mp3 audio podcasts that are out there. There are lots of podcasts available from the iTunes store, so that's a handy place to find and subscribe to them.

Remember, time management works a little bit differently for everyone, but if you remember to take notes, streamline, and use your time wisely, you'll see your time management—and outlook—improve.

Taking the "Dis" out of Disadvantage

There are many ways that contemporary office culture can rob us of productive time. Meetings, conflict resolutions, marketing research, unexpected emergencies—the modern office is a jungle with lots of ambushes waiting in the tall grass. Any use of your time that isn't controlled directly by you is a problem and a disadvantage. Here are some of my favorite methods to turn these disadvantages in my favor.

1. **Use deadlines and protected times.** Dedicate chunks of protected time to the important tasks. So if your most important task is calling ABC client, pin it on your calendar so you dedicate time to make sure that it gets done and that time isn't used for two or three other things.

2. **Go to someone else's office to meet.** This works because you control the time. If somebody comes into my office, they put me in a position where I have to wait them out (they control the time) or I have to end the conversation, which isn't as easy to do gracefully. If I go into their office, I control the time, which means I can get what I need out of the interaction and then end it positively and gracefully.

3. **Turn off your phone.** Your phone is such a distraction. However, as in my industry, if turning off the phone isn't possible because you're on call 24/7, just program the phone to use a different audio alert for clients. That way,

instead of you checking your e-mail every few minutes, the alert will tell you if you need to respond immediately. And if you aren't on call, add an out-of-the-office assistant to your e-mail and turn off your phone.

4. **Put up the "Do Not Disturb" sign.** We do this in our company. We ask our recruiters, when they're working on certain projects, to put "Do Not Disturb" on their phones, close their doors, and put "Do Not Disturb" signs out there too—and we respect this. If you have to do it, people will understand. It's about getting your job done. That's why we're all at work, right? If you want, you can personalize your message or autoresponder with "I'll get back to you as soon as I drain this swamp," or something like that. Add humor where you can and people will respond in kind.

5. **Close the blinds.** Turn off the lights. Lock the door. In fact, *leave the office.* I do my best work from home. Or if you're feeling completely stressed out, don't stay at your desk and growl like a crazy person. Go take a walk for fifteen minutes, clear your brain, come back, and refocus. If you're at work, make sure you're fully present.

6. **Your professional life? It's nothing personal.** Stay focused at work. When I was a newly appointed recruiter at Remedy, my grandpa passed away. He had cancer, but we didn't think he would pass as suddenly as he did. I was traumatized. I had just started as a recruiter. I took the day off for the funeral and forced myself to go back to work the next day. I took a day to grieve—and every evening and weekend after that, outside work. Of course, I was distraught, but work didn't stop. There was a reason I

had the position I had. It was because they needed that position filled with a responsible, productive person. Life takes turns every day and at any moment. But your job demands consistency and dependability. If you're hit with a serious surprise, seek help outside work—a grievance counselor, friends, and so on. You're not cold or heartless if you take only a day off. Strong emotional intelligence is the best support you can have. So turn disaster into new energy. Transfer your pain, frustration, and heartbreak into determination. Focus that energy on excelling in your career, improving, and helping others. Any time I go through a tough situation, I turn to work to help me get over it quickly. The trick is to realign your passion so you can use it to move ahead.

Three Smartt Ways to Guard Your Protected Time

It's up to you to take your schedule seriously and guard it jealously. Here are three ways to do that:

1. Block out hours on your calendar, weeks or even months in advance. If one to three p.m. is a great productive time for you, keep it that way by putting a fence around it on your calendar, even if it means you have to add an hour to your workday.

2. Always ask for calendar invitations whenever you can. Send them when you can. If you receive one, feel free to suggest alterations that work around your protected hours.

3. Mark protected time on your e-mail signature. If one to three p.m. is off-limits, just say so.

Smartt Steps

1. Schedule smart. Take advantage of geographic locations, other obligations on your calendar, and your most productive times of day.

2. Cut down or cut out the meaningless noise and the time sinks in your life. TV, gossip, and staring at the Internet for hours isn't bettering anyone or getting things done.

3. Learn to say no to distractions.

   - Turn off all but the essential notifications.
   - Schedule times to check your email, work group chat, or other potential distractions. Make your scheduled check times known so that expectations are managed.

4. Stick to your schedule.

5. Cultivate focus. Silence your phone, close the office door, and don't be afraid of the "Do Not Disturb" sign.

"So much depends on our attitude. The way we choose to see things and respond to others makes all the difference."

THOMAS MONSON

STEP THREE

Adopt a Positive Attitude to Achieve Positive Results

I was let go from Remedy when I was a receptionist. It had never happened to me before, but the office was not doing very well, so the owners, Nadine and Carl, decided to close it. Suddenly, Cathy, the office manager, and I were out of a job. It came abruptly, and I was shocked. I could have become self-critical or taken it out on Nadine and Carl, but I didn't. Instead, I held my head high and thanked them for the opportunity. I was unemployed for two long weeks until I finally received a call from Cathy. Nadine and Carl's last remaining branch needed a recruiter, and she got me the job. Now imagine that I'd gone out with an attitude and all grumpy and hurt. They very likely wouldn't have offered me that second opportunity. Maintaining a positive attitude is essential if you want to achieve great success. No one knows better than your coworkers how hard you work. They know you won't let them down. This loyalty can last for years, so even if a first opportunity doesn't pan out, remain professional and friendly and trust that your good connections will prove fruitful in the end.

Turn Negativity on Its Head

Negative people feed and energize me. My competitive nature compels me to prove to people that they're wrong *about me*. If you're like me, you've had people in your life who have said, "You'll never do that. You're not clever enough. You're not smart enough. You'll never own a company." Silence your critics by ignoring them outwardly, while saying to yourself inwardly, "I'll show them!" Turn their negativity on its head and use it to drive your determination. Let your successes speak for you. You know what you're capable of, and you are capable of greatness (yes, *you!*).

Positive Power

Positivity is one of the most important markers for happy, effective, productive people. Positivity doesn't mean everything is going great. Often, it's just the opposite. But **operating with a positive attitude is essential to success.** Positivity helps you work from a solution-finding point of view. Positivity's cousin, confidence, reduces strain on your coworkers, family, and friends.

You Determine Your Reality

The biggest difference between a positive and a negative attitude is perspective. If you come to the table with blame swirling around in your head, you're probably avoiding your part in the situation. But if you come with a positive outlook, seeking solutions instead of where to place the blame, your confidence will shine through. That kind of attitude can spread like wildfire, helping the whole team work together to improve a situation.

If we spent all of our days focused on the anguish, disappointment, and negativity in the world around us to the exclusion of all else, we'd stop showing up. We'd all stay in bed, under the covers. Simple as that. Positivity helps us become energized and empowered, qualities that are essential to getting in front of a problem and making a difference.

Start Your Day Strong

It's important to do a few essential things every morning. These are not complicated things. They're the basic things we all need to do as humans. Stretch, drink water, and eat something if you're hungry. (But don't force it; everybody's different!) In addition to the fundamentals, these habits will also help you start your day off right:

- Make to-do lists and then look over your list for the day and review your plan of attack.
- If you don't make lists, take five to ten minutes to let your mind focus on what you would like to accomplish.
- Think about ways you can make space in the day to be productive and positive.
- Finally, think about how to allow yourself room to be effective at whatever you have to do.

On Really Tough Days, Go for "Positivity Overload"

Some days we all just need a little extra: extra support from friends or coworkers, an extra luxury, or something as simple as an unusually fancy coffee drink. I like to use books, music, uplifting podcasts, and videos to inspire me if I'm feeling low. Inspirational quotes and TED Talks can help shift your perspective. And if you really need the "big guns," go to YouTube and search for "faith in humanity restored." Some kind, forward-thinking people have created compilation videos of people being great to each other (and to other living creatures) that are sure to pump you back up.

Mastering Your Emotions

Reflection is important in understanding your core values, but you also need to know how to handle yourself in situations that are unpleasant or stressful.

When we get upset, it's hard to act logically and reasonably. Knowing your triggers will help you become a better person and help you respond instead of react.

Triggers 101

Believe it or not, I've actually taken a class on recognizing triggers and what to do with them. It was interesting to find out many people's triggers are similar. In the world of work, a common trigger is being cut off in conversation. In meetings with several people in the room, people tend to cut each other off in conversation and it can be *very* frustrating. It could be that emotions are running hot and the atmosphere is stressful, or it may be that everyone's excited to dig in and solve a problem. The result is that certain people go unheard while the more outspoken run the conversation. Team members who feel they're being ignored or rejected often internalize their frustration at such treatment and later vent that frustration in other areas of work. It is not an empowering feeling to be bowled over in conversation.

Managing other people's triggers is impossible if you don't know what they are. I'm not necessarily suggesting that you sit one-on-one with each of your team members to find out what their triggers are, but you could try to pay more attention to see if a pattern surfaces. And the same, of course, applies to you. Learn your own triggers and take steps to keep them at bay. If, for instance, you feel your views are being ignored, you are better off letting your team know. Persistence may be necessary. The important part is to recognize how you *react* in certain situations so you can choose to respond instead.

It's also good to **be on the lookout for poor choices that become bad habits**. Biting your nails is one example. A lot of people think it's a bad habit. To break the habit, you must learn to notice when you're doing it, which is really hard because you do it without thinking. Breaking and preventing bad habits require self-awareness. Once you've gained that insight, though, it doesn't take very long to train yourself to respond in new, healthy ways.

For example, it's hard for me to get gym time into my schedule, but once I do and I get into my routine, it becomes an automatic part of my day. **Practice making good things a habit.**

Know Your Limits

Be aware of when you're overextending yourself. You can do anything, but you can't do *everything*. I do feel bad saying no sometimes, but I also know that I can't do everything. I'm in touch with my body, which helps. When I've done too much, I can feel my body saying, "Get some sleep!" Your body will send you similar signals too if you're listening.

Remember Gratitude

Being grateful is an essential part of staying positive on both good days and bad. Feeling grateful is only half of the recipe, though; *sharing* that gratitude is the other half. If a coworker does something for you (even if it was you who requested it), say "thank you." It's easy, simple, good manners and goes a lot further than you might think. Gratitude is an infectious thing, and when your team feels your gratitude, their gratitude comes pouring back. In this way, *you* can be the rising tide that raises the positivity across your whole business.

Garbage in, Garbage Out

Try not to get stuck in the garbage cycle. Eat good, healthy food, and you get healthy energy. Think positive, problem-solving thoughts, and you'll get better solutions. Think "I can" in place of "I can't," and consider what's possible instead of all the things that might be impossible. A fun exercise: any time you catch yourself saying or thinking "I can't," turn it on its head right then and there. Think through the scenario, assuming it is possible. You might be surprised at how often you find a solution during this exercise, or at least some viable courses of action. Remember, you're a work in progress. We all are! Remembering to focus on the positivity around you can help you keep your mind from negative, energy-stealing spaces. Negative in, negative out. Don't dwell on bad information. Focus on learning, growing, and improving!

Five Ways to Neutralize Negative People

Negativity is like sand. It can creep into every aspect of our lives if we let it. It can come from so many places and for so many reasons that sometimes it seems that failure is inevitable. We all have to deal with people who say, "You'll never make it." Maybe it's their fear of failure, or maybe it's simple jealousy. But remember, they're just making it up. They have no proof that you're going to fail. They just have negative comments. But you have the power; you can ignore them and make their comments meaningless—because if you listen to them, you will start to believe them.

Five Ways to Neutralize Negativity

1. **Empathize.** This one, simple exercise alone can make a world of difference. There's a phrase that makes the rounds from time to time in various forms: "Everyone has a struggle you can't see." Allow for the possibility that the negativity you're experiencing is the symptom of a problem that's invisible on the surface. When you choose to empathize, your own tension drops. Your ability to put yourself in someone else's shoes (even in the case of an unknown problem) sets you up as an automatic advocate. (And it gets you out of the immediate line of fire.) Empathizing, by the way, doesn't mean you commit to fixing the other person's problems. It's a state of mind you embrace to neutralize negativity.

2. **Praise the positive.** This is essential. Do it whenever you can. Even in the darkest of moments, call out the good. Negativity spreads in the shadows but vanishes in the light.

3. **Don't stoop to argue.** We've all felt, at times, that when we encounter negativity, our only option is to respond with more negativity. It can be challenging, but don't give in to the urge to argue or insult. Agree to disagree if you must, but you probably won't have to. It can be very helpful to reset everything by simply saying, "Okay, we are where we are. Now, how do we solve the problem?"

4. **Look for solutions-based conversations.** When you're beset by problems and surrounded by negativity, change the

subject and start talking about solutions. It's too easy to say, "Oh no! It's all over!" Instead try, "What are our options? What can we do?" Just asking these simple questions can cause a whole range of positive alternatives to appear.

5. **Don't focus on blame.** As gratifying as it can be to look for the person or event to blame for a negative outcome, it's not really productive. Instead, look ahead to the next step. In the short term, focus on looking for actions that will neutralize or fix the situation. If someone really does need to be held accountable, deal with it after the immediate threat has passed, when you can use it as a teaching or learning experience.

There's no real way to ignore negativity in the world, in work, or in our personal lives. Remember to empathize and avoid arguments wherever possible. Frame things in a positive way by looking for solutions, not blame. That will neutralize negativity and produce a positive outcome from a negative event.

Bonus: you'll be seen as a problem solver, which will help you build your reputation as a leader.

Being New to the Team

When I accepted the recruiter position and joined the Santa Rosa team, I joined a group of people who were already friends and had tons of experience working together. I had very little work experience and definitely no recruiting experience. I embraced the opportunity. If you find yourself in a similar situation, be friendly and outgoing and work hard to show that you're a team player. Make sure you participate in meetings and be generous with your comments and actions. You will rise to the occasion and prove to yourself and others that you belong there.

Don't Underestimate Yourself

You can accomplish the unthinkable. It's often in moments of fear and panic that people can grow the most.

Those Who Embrace and Initiate Change Will Thrive

Change is inevitable and accepting that change will happen is vital to the health of your professional life. The sooner you realize this, the more quickly you'll be on the road to success. Today, it's fashionable to talk about disruption, another word for change. People are realizing that **without change, we never learn, and there are so many different ways to learn from change and challenges.** Try to visualize where you think the change will take you and turn yourself in that direction. In other words, go with the flow into uncharted territories, having faith in your ability to learn and thrive. Obviously, not everything turns out perfectly. But you will always learn a lot along the way.

If you run across an opportunity or are handed an assignment that is totally foreign to you, give yourself a moment to feel excited about it. Think about it: you've started from zero on every single thing you have ever tried. Is the situation in front of you an opportunity to grow? Will you learn a new and valuable set of skills from taking the opportunity?

Know your limits and push them. Only you know how much you can take on, but I bet it's more than you think. It's like doing that last rep at the gym. If you put your mind to doing thirty reps, and you get to twenty-eight, nine times out of ten, you'll be able to complete the last two. The same goes for making those last two calls or connections in a day, or finishing a report, or going to that networking dinner even though what you really want is to curl up in front of the television in your pajamas. The pajamas will still be there—the opportunity won't. Take care of yourself, of course, but take care of opportunity too.

Turn Threats into Opportunities: How to Stay Positive When Faced with Change and Uncertainty

Change doesn't always mean bad news. In fact, it may mean new opportunities. Here are four opportunities to see you through times of impending change:

1. **The New Boss.** The new boss scenario is often the biggest shake-up. You finally get the old boss figured out, when, oops, somebody new shows up. Not knowing what to expect in terms of new workflows, plans, strategies, and expectations can feel pretty threatening.

   - **Take your time.** Don't assume! Evaluate the situation and give the new boss time to move into his/her new role and to explicitly state new expectations. Allow both your new boss and yourself time to make sense of the new environment before even entertaining the idea of panic.
   - **If you have questions, ask them.** Don't let anxieties build up and cripple you.
   - **Look for good news.** Sometimes, change is so emotionally negative that you don't see what's good

even if it hits you in the head. A new boss doesn't have to shake up your day-to-day routine. And if your routine is changed, be grateful. Time to wake up!

2.   **The Acquisition/Merger.** Your first thought: "I might be let go." In most cases, during an acquisition or merger, pretty much everyone's in the same boat. Unless your position is crucial to your company's operations and you're the only one around who can do it (whether that means skills or training or both), everyone's position could be under threat, theoretically. Remember, this could be positive news. Have good faith.

   - **First: don't sweat it.** Sweating it doesn't fix anything and won't prevent what might feel like impending doom.
   - **Second: perform at your optimum level.** Don't feel the need to give the new boss the red carpet treatment; just do your job well. Communicate with your coworkers. Put your natural best foot forward.
   - **Third: you're not alone.** Remember, everyone around you is probably feeling uncertain too. Support your coworkers and tap into that unified front that makes your group so effective. Operate there, surrounded by your teammates, not alone and from a place of fear.
   - **Fourth: there really is a bright side.** If the worst really does come to pass, it will at least change your situation, and that might be good. As some pretty

smart people have said of many scary transitional situations, "This, or something better."

3. **The New Client.** This challenge is, perhaps, just as likely to be an exciting, positive "threat" as a negative one. New clients can shake things up if you aren't prepared (and sometimes even when you are very well prepared).

    - **Make a plan.** Discuss within your company how far you're willing to bend with new clients. They can sometimes ask for big, overwhelming changes to the services you provide or how you conduct business. They can disrupt workflow. They can demand things that would be unprofitable or unwise. Having a plan beforehand helps to manage expectations without weathering a scramble phase.

    - **Hear them out.** New clients can also be tremendous resources, bringing outside perspectives to your services and processes, so give them an ear. Don't feel compelled to say yes to everything they suggest! Don't be afraid to say, "That's on our roadmap for the future, but we don't do it now." Make sure their expectations match your capabilities.

4. **The New Hire.** New people can be scary.

    - **Don't be intimidated.** Unless they're made of stone, those new people are just as nervous as you are.

    - **Don't worry too much about making fast friends.** Instead, be receptive and warm, but give new colleagues room to come to you. Some people call this behavior "holding space." In part, it's designed to lower the overall anxiety between people. You're essentially giving new hires permission to get comfortable with the situation on their own terms.

The Most Important Question to Ask Yourself

Always, both in your personal and your professional life, ask yourself, "How can I improve?" In the short term and in the long term, what could you be doing better? Could something you're working on be done cheaper or more efficiently? After all, any cost savings is beneficial to the company. Employers love that. Remember, small solutions can produce big changes.

For example, a major airline asked employees what ideas they had to reduce costs. One of the baggage handlers said, "Why not offer passengers one olive in their martinis instead of the four olives we've been giving?" Implementing that one idea saved the airline hundreds of thousands of dollars, and the passengers likely didn't feel like they were missing out.

Confidence Counts

Don't be intimidated. As Facebook's Sheryl Sandberg points out in her book *Lean In*, come to the table, sit at the table, and answer the questions you're asked.

Since They Asked . . .

A lot of companies have suggestion boxes. Provide your suggestions, but make sure they're good. Do your research. Don't just instantly say, "Kool-Aid dispensers are a great idea" because you like that beverage. Do some homework. *Why* is it a good idea? Put time into it.

Think of "Teamly" Solutions

As the saying goes, "Many hands make light work." After decades of management theories revolving around internal competition, more companies are emphasizing collaboration more than competition, which is *huge*. You might be competing for top ranking, but your company needs you to be part of a cohesive team, so embrace not only your drive and determination but also your ability to help others succeed. **You can't get to the top by yourself. There's no way. Even if you, personally, work your butt off, you are always part of a team.** There are people who help you in various ways to get to the top. Your job, now, is to get them to want to help you stay there and *succeed*.

Don't Defeat Yourself

Don't start saying, "Gosh, I'm not good at this. I'm not the best for this project. I can't do it." You're only making excuses. Even when you don't succeed, you can't just close up shop and call it a day. Michael Jordan didn't make the varsity basketball team in his sophomore year of high school, but despite that fact, he became one of the most celebrated NBA Hall of Famers. Oprah Winfrey was publicly fired from her first television job as an anchor for "getting too emotionally invested in her stories," but she rebounded and became the undisputed queen of television, worth an estimated $3 billion, according to *Forbes* magazine. Vera Wang failed to make the 1968 US Olympics figure-skating team. She then became an editor at *Vogue* but was passed over for the editor-in-chief position. So she began designing wedding gowns at age forty!

When things don't go our way, it's easy to feel defeated. In trying times, it's important to remember that the most successful people don't let failure keep them down. They keep their chin up, learn from their experiences, and look for a silver lining.

Smartt Steps

1. Be solutions oriented. Do a "can't" audit. For a week or two, write down every time you think or say, "I can't do that" or, "I can't make that happen." Then, when you have time to do so, sit down with that list and play devil's advocate. See how many potential solutions to the problem you can come up with.

2. Cultivate self-awareness so you can train yourself out of bad habits and into good ones. Realizing that you're repeating a habit you consider bad or negative is the first opportunity to choose a different response. It's key to not get bogged down in blaming yourself. Just note it, observe it, and begin preparing to respond in a more true-to-you way next time.

3. Practice empathy. Step into other people's shoes, and consider things from their perspective. Remember, we never really know someone else's story.

4. Allow yourself to change and grow. Get excited about new material and unfamiliar territory. Entertain the idea that you are up to the challenge.

"Make yourself indispensable. The more valuable you are,
the more responsibility you will be asked to take on."
FRAN HAUSER

STEP FOUR

Become an Information Junkie

I never finished college, okay? There, I said it. I took some classes at a community college, but that was it. College was history. And I can't say I regret it. Sure, I missed out on traditional classes and social relationships with professors and classmates, but during those four years, I worked—and I have to say I feel I've benefited greatly from the real-world lessons I learned during those "college years."

I couldn't afford college, but I loved learning. **It's important, whether you go to school or you don't, that you keep learning.** The world is in a constant state of change, led by technology. The business world is not immune: every shop, every office, every factory is being rattled by change. If you're not ahead of the curve or at least up to date, you're going to fall behind.

For birthdays, I give my friends self-help books filled with advice on how to succeed and triumph. Learning and growing is a critical part of success. So I read, and when I'm driving, I listen to audio books. If you're listening to an audio version of a book or reading it in print, I congratulate you because you know it's important to develop yourself and to constantly grow, not only as a person but professionally—and to make every minute count. When I took on my first recruiting position, I read books about how to be a recruiter, how to be a manager, how to be a better leader, and, of course, how to make sales. College degree or not, you too can become an information junkie. You cannot be successful without reading, so invest in yourself.

Get the Right Textbooks on Your List

One of my *aha!* moments came when I read a book by Jeffrey Gitomer, a sales expert and another successful person who didn't graduate from college. In fact, *The Charlotte Observer* describes him as "a college dropout who has built a sales-training empire." He makes the point that sales is really about the relationship-building aspect of a job. I read his book and learned lessons that have guided me through to this day. One of the things I learned is that great books can give you exceptional support. So part of my educational program is to read more and more. It pays to pick the brains of the best!

The Smartt List of Books

1. *Never Eat Alone* by **Keith Ferrazzi**. Your network is your net worth. This book shows you how to add to your personal bottom line by connecting more skillfully.

2. *StrengthsFinder 2.0* by **Tom Rath**. This book will change the way you look at yourself—and the world around you.

3. *Little Red Book of Selling* by **Jeffrey Gitomer**. As CEOs or receptionists, we are all

in the business of selling, regardless of our title.

4. *Little Teal Book of Trust* by Jeffrey Gitomer. Read this for a lifetime of growth and success as you seek to understand and master the principles of trust.

5. *Wrestling with Success* by Nikita Koloff and Jeffrey Gitomer. This book shows readers how to prepare themselves for any challenge in life and attain ultimate success.

6. *Lean In* by Sheryl Sandberg. This book is an inspiring call to action and a blueprint for individual growth.

7. *Life Is Tremendous* by Charles "Tremendous" Jones. This timeless little book is my absolute favorite and is a great read for anyone who wants to learn to really live.

8. *12 Pillars of Success* by Jim Rohn and Chris Widener. The principles of success in a quick, easy, and fun format. I highly recommend this one too.

9. *What Motivates Me* by Adrian Gostick and Chester Elton. A great strategy: find what truly motivates you and align it with the work you do every day, for the rest of your life.

10. *Little Gold Book of Yes! Attitude* by Jeffrey Gitomer. All business winners have one thing in common: a "Yes! Attitude"—one that's powerful enough to help achieve the impossible.

A great reading list provides knowledge you can take with you. I went from receptionist to recruiter to business services manager. Nobody sat down with me and formally trained me. I just approached *everyone* as a mentor, and if they weren't accessible, I read their books!

When I was a recruiter, I was asked to manage Direct Hire, a division of Remedy Staffing that placed CEOs, accountants, and executive assistants to the CEO. And so here I was, without a degree, speaking to people with MBAs. I was nervous and thought that my lack of a college degree may have caught up with me. Instead of letting the doubts progress, I reminded myself that I was in that role for a reason and that the owners had confidence in me to take on that responsibility. This was no time for a pity party. I began researching great interview questions for the types of positions we were filling and overcame my jitters with the help of a mentor.

Seek Mentors

Great mentors can be found in a variety of places, so try looking outside your current workplace. Seek out mentors at business and women's associations in your area, nonprofit organizations, within your family, church groups, and even community groups such as chambers of commerce.

Learn Daily

Whether you're reading articles written by thought leaders in your field or learning how to refinish a table, keep learning. It helps your brain stay flexible and can help you make connections faster.

Top Five Lessons I've learned from Watching Others

1. **Overwork doesn't mean better work.** Taking on every challenge doesn't equal automatic success. Attacking every available obstacle, accepting every challenge—these things don't always make you a better person. If you feel you're edging toward burnout, stop and take the time to evaluate your position. Remember, don't work yourself to the point of losing your drive.

2. **Sacrifices are part of success.** Out of all the key essentials, this one was the toughest for me. We all have to make sacrifices to get what we want. And, of course, it's important to have a work/life balance, but I missed out on many friends' events to work at home or attend networking events and build my brand. Starting a company is like starting a family: it's a complex, lifetime commitment. Any commitment that big requires discipline. Are you ready to make the sacrifice?

3. **Delegate.** There are likely people on your team who are great at some of the tasks you're facing. Managing resources means managing the people who make the business run well. Give them responsibilities; watch and encourage them as they meet those responsibilities. Don't be afraid to let go of things. Biting off more than you can chew can be detrimental to the work's quality, to your sense of well-being, to your company's success and, ultimately, to your happiness and satisfaction.

4. **Know that it's not always the early bird that gets the worm.** It's always the tenacious one. If you fail, try again. Give meaning and importance to failure, not just to success. Keep trying. Keep improving. Keep learning. Stay with the problem, and work to conquer the insurmountable. The result will be success.

5. **Use all the tools in your shed.** I don't learn only from mentors. I take stock of all the resources at my disposal— and there are more of those now than ever.

    - **Blogs.** I always enjoy learning little gems from social media. I follow inspirational blogs such as SUCCESS (www.success.com), Darren Hardy (darrenhardy.success.com), and Jeffrey Gitomer's Sales Blog (www.salesblog.com).

    - **Twitter.** If you're not already using Twitter for professional growth, a great way to begin is to follow people you look up to and read their inspirational tweets. If you follow the right people, you can learn a surprising amount from their focused and thoughtful 140-character tidbits about working efficiently, presenting yourself professionally, and positioning yourself to succeed in business. Twitter chats are another great way to connect with and learn from influential businesspeople.

    - **LinkedIn.** Identify and follow influencers who reflect the individual you want to be. I learned the value of personal branding from a variety of social media platforms, but I think exceptional personal branding is best demonstrated on platforms such as LinkedIn. Use professional endorsements and recommendations to call out the buzzwords you want reflected in your personal brand.

- **Pinterest.** Yes, Pinterest! Don't be surprised. Pinterest isn't just for creating a vision board or shopping; it contains valuable content from many sources, and its interface allows you to easily find what you're looking for. Plus, no hashtags needed.

You can learn *tons* from others about succeeding in business. Where better to learn from others than by carefully using the right online tools?

Everything Is Outside the Box You're In

Why does your growth and development matter? It's essential to challenge and stretch yourself often and not let yourself get stuck in a job where you don't feel you're growing or learning.

You Are the Tip of Your Own Iceberg

There is more potential in each of us than we know. It's a fast-paced world with everyone wanting it all *now*, in real time, and the world is constantly evolving, so it's more important than ever to continue to grow professionally *and* personally. Not only does intentional growth and development have the potential to make you better at your job, but it can help you feel more fulfilled both in and out of the workplace.

Five Smartt Ways to Think Outside the Box

1. **Take on new challenges.** Take a deep breath and jump. Doing new things and thinking about stuff in a new way can be risky, stressful, and sometimes confusing. But it's better than remaining stuck. Understanding risk is how professionals and successful companies survive. Sometimes, it may seem that new problems crop up as fast as you solve the old ones (sometimes faster), but that just means you are moving, and you are getting better and stronger.

2. **Read.** Yep, read that again—without moving your lips—because it's really that straightforward! Read informative articles from solid, respected sources. (If there are citations, you're going in the right direction.) Pick up a book, in electronic or print format, or take an online class, or just reread the beginning of this chapter!

3. **Invest in your learning.** There are many free webinars on practically every subject imaginable. Carve out some time each day (or each week) to watch a webinar or two. Most are short, easy to understand, and don't take huge pieces out of your already busy life. Or take a whole course! I love Coursera for learning online, but there are many options, both free and paid.

4. **Get a mentor.** Look within your company for someone to mentor you. If no one is available internally, try www.FindAMentor.com, or ask your colleagues for other recommendations.

5.   **Surround yourself with like-minded peers.** See if there are Meetup groups in your area. Make friends, collaborate, and have fun. It's guaranteed to be enriching.

There is always **something** you can improve on. Make daily deposits into your personal-development bank, and soon your bank account will grow.

You Are Here

What you bring to your position can be so much more than what's evident on your resume. Reading online, reading articles about your industry, listening to podcasts, and taking webinars will build your personal cache of knowledge and expand your abilities. Don't limit yourself to the narrow confines of the job that's been handed to you. There are so many avenues and resources for us to use to better ourselves as workers and as people that it would be a shame to not take advantage of them. With the Internet, everything is quickly accessible, so no excuses! Just take it one step at a time, starting where you are, even if that's at the bottom. Starting at the bottom in an entry-level position may take longer, but the benefits are endless. By the time you reach the top, you will know all the positions from the bottom up. That kind of education will make you a stronger, wiser leader.

Five Things You Can Learn in Complete Silence

1.   **Pick up artistic skills.** A little bit of basic graphic design goes a long way. If you spend time even doodling, you're also exercising different parts of your brain that can help you perform better at seemingly unrelated tasks.

2. **Master any subject you didn't get a chance to learn in school.** So much information is just a mouse click away. Make use of it by following up on any of your thoughts that start with "I wonder how . . ."

Bonus tip: learning about many different subjects, even just a small amount, keeps your creativity flowing and your brain flexible.

3. **Get your hands dirty.** Working with your hands can have a profoundly de-stressing effect on you. Don't know how to make anything with your hands? That's okay; you can learn. Plus, it feels wonderful to look at something you've made with your hands and say, "I made that." Especially if you see it in a craft shop the next week with a $100 price tag on it.

4. **Learn to code.** A beautifully designed webpage is a handmade object. You can take courses online, read about different philosophies regarding programming style, or just learn how to use HTML. You might be surprised at how well you adapt and how much of your regular Internet usage makes more sense with just a little bit of a programming background. And I'll tell you this: learning to code certainly won't make you less valuable to current or potential employers.

5. **You can learn a wealth of information about yourself.** If you cultivate silence and make space for learning, you'll probably discover you have a whole lot more self-discipline than you thought. You'll learn that the world around you

is often noisy and can cut out many of the ideas that come quietly. Think about how often people have ingenious ideas while standing in the shower or while walking to the mailbox. One of those people is you.

Smartt Steps

1. Make time for learning. Spend an hour a day learning and improving.

2. Make daily reading a habit. Purchase one of the books from "The Smartt List of Books," and begin growing your personal development bank.

3. Give yourself a challenge. Next time you say, "I can't" or, "I don't think I can," stop and think about all the ways you can achieve it. Remember, we all start at a zero skill level for everything in life. Just because you currently don't have that skill set doesn't mean you'll never get there.

4. As you learn more, show your boss that you're capable of doing more. Volunteer for a project that's outside your normal scope of responsibilities and ace it!

"The most important connections you make in life are the connections you make with others."
TOM FORD

STEP FIVE

Cultivate and Nurture Your Network

When Nadine and Carl sold their business to a larger competitor, I was asked to become a sales representative. The company believed every office should have a sales rep to bring in new business. I took the position and quickly realized what a busy and saturated marketplace it was. There were twenty-three other staffing firms in the area. One sales rep I was going up against had been in the industry for thirteen-plus years and was with a nearby, well-established company that owned the local market. Here I was with a newly named company and no background in sales besides my retail experience. But I wanted to dominate. I wanted to be the best. I had made it this far. I wasn't going to let intimidation get the best of me. Competition was strong, but I *knew* as long as I worked hard and spent every waking hour improving, no one could beat me. They weren't spending the time as I was, pounding the pavement and building relationships. All that time paid off. My network grew and grew and so did my reputation. In less than two years, I was making a name for myself—and the company.

A Network Is Your Social Ecology

As you grow, personally and professionally, so will your friendships. In high school, I gravitated toward friends with common interests: sports, academics, and a sense of fun. In looking back from where I am now, my life has changed, and so have my values and my career. There is great beauty in having old friends. However, throughout my life, my friends have changed over time as I have changed.

As you grow, you need to ensure the people you're surrounding yourself with reflect a constant arc of improvement and progress. Assess your friends list to determine if they are still having a positive impact on your life. Do your friends bring out the best in you or the worst? Do they bring you down or inspire you? Do they provide encouragement and reinforcement when you've lost your way?

When I became a recruiter, I had set hours and a commitment to my employer. At the same time, my friends were in college and enjoying the flexible schedule and the house-party scene. I couldn't keep up with that life and my professional life, so I began to distance myself. While it was tough to make that change—and trust me when I say "tough," because these were my best friends—it was the right decision for me and my career. You have to put yourself first when it comes to your priorities and your goals. This was the first of many hard decisions ahead.

Gifts from Friends

Friendship is a beautiful gift. **If you want greatness in your life, then you need to surround yourself with great people.** If your goal is to become a better person, a smarter person, a more fulfilled person, then surround yourself with individuals who possess those qualities. Don't be afraid to befriend people you admire, people smarter than you, people you want to emulate. If they become true friends, their best qualities will rub off on you. Stretch yourself to be among peers who can and will grow with you as time goes on but who won't hold you back or bring you down.

Choose Wisely

Keep friends who motivate and inspire you, friends who have a clear direction and are motivated themselves. It's not being selfish or heartless. It's being true to yourself and the person you want to become. The easiest way to lose track of your goals is to surround yourself with the wrong people. You don't have to expel them from your life. You can still love them all you want, but don't let them prevent you from allowing new people into your inner circle.

Life Is Not a Soap Opera

Cut out the drama. In order to do this, you need to be honest with your friends about the type of individual you are. Don't try to convince them. Show them. Drama comes to those who love drama. As soon as I started separating myself from drama-filled friends, my life got quiet quickly. My true friendships have a kind of purity that I cherish. In order to not attract drama, you must not spread or engage in the chitchat that one would associate with it. Don't feed the weaknesses in others that contribute to it. By surrounding myself with strong women and men, I'm able to invest my energy in my career. Think about the time it takes to listen, tell, or react to negative conversations. And don't forget the drain on your energy! **A friend is never a burden weighing you down. A friend constantly lifts you up.**

Relationships Start with Conversations

Remain authentic. Don't try to play a role. Stay true to your values. Be honest and transparent in your communication. Speak clearly, confidently, and from the heart. Building strong relationships starts with strong communication.

Finding Like-Minded Peers

There are many places you can go to find friends with common interests. You can go to a Meetup group, a chamber function, or an affiliate group that speaks to your mind. Think about alternatives too, such as a book club or a charity organization. Consider sitting on a board to gain access to an executive management team.

When seeking out people with common interests, think about the benefits of diversity. I have a wide array of friends and acquaintances who make my network not only bigger than most but also deeper and wider. The reason: they're from all walks of life. Not only is this great for business, but it's also great for me. I'm constantly exposed to new ways of thinking and learning. I look for trailblazers leading the pack. These people are, typically, in management roles, and their thinking and actions make them interesting to follow and emulate. Look for people who are in a role similar to yours. They know the struggles you're experiencing because they have been there. And watch for friends who are looking to reach the top but are new to the career world. They represent an opportunity for you to mentor someone else.

The Power of Networks

If you want to be successful, networking is the difference between mediocre and *big*. One of my biggest assets is my generous, exciting, and interesting network. Think of it as a beautiful garden. You sow the seeds and nurture their growth. As you would in your garden, you need to weed, trim, and prune your network to keep it healthy and vibrant. And like your garden, your network needs to be fed. You do that by exposing your peers to great ideas and bright thinkers. Every member of your network has the potential to bloom.

I've been watering the seeds of my network for years, and I'm starting to reap serious benefits. The reason is simple: relationships are the bread and butter of success. We need people to buy our products or services, and vice versa. The more connected you are, the more resources you will have access to, and the easier your success will come. Make a point to get connected and stay connected. Everyone knows someone. Word of mouth is the fastest and easiest way to build your business, your brand—and your bank account!

Networks Become Self-Supporting

Building your network as early as possible helps so much later in life. It makes your job easier. When you have a large, diverse network, you're able to pull from it. In my job, my network has helped me bring in new clients each week without a sales pitch. It has also helped me create stronger relationships and has won me awards. The time invested in building and nurturing your network will pay off big.

Be a Superconnector

People sometimes forget that you don't become successful overnight. It took years for me to get to the point I'm at now. Connections sometimes take years to pay off, but when they do, the payoff can be huge. Connect people to other people. It's been one of the foundations of my success. When I meet someone new, I am always thinking of people I know whom they should know. Help others, and it will be returned to you.

Every lunch is an opportunity to connect with new people and learn about them. To this day, I have a meeting with somebody new once a week.

Networks Help You Polish Your Reputation

Just as in all other things, practice makes perfect. Helping others make valuable connections, even when you aren't directly benefiting from it, strengthens and hones your reputation. Eventually, you won't have to work so hard to convince people you're the right fit for what they need (if you actually are); your reputation can take care of that.

The Lunch-Hour Network Strategy

Successful networks can be built around a lunch hour. I started my lunch-hour networking practice about five years ago and have seen a huge spike in stronger relationships. Everybody eats lunch, so I decided to use the time for something more than soup and sandwiches. I schedule three lunch meetings a week, and I use that time to connect with other people and see how I can help each of them. That's always my goal when meeting people: I want to know how I can help them by asking thoughtful questions. It turns out that's also a great way for me to learn. Put lunch meetings on your calendar to build stronger relationships with people you've just met or people you've already met but want to know better.

Face-to-Face versus Social Interactions

Social media is increasingly popular, but I still believe face-to-face interaction is the best. Start by becoming a leader in your local community: join the local chamber of commerce or the board of a local nonprofit organization. You need both face-to-face and social-media interactions to be at the top of your game. Each platform will help you achieve greatness and take your career to new heights with the right plan.

Top Seven Kinds of Organizations That Have Positively Impacted My Career

The goal here is to be a leader, not just a member. So participate. Share your ideas. Utilize your network. Spread your wings—and your influence.

1. **Chamber of commerce events.** These are tried and true. While most groups have their cliques, there are always important people here. It's also a great place for you to practice your introductions and networking. It takes time and practice to perfect your thirty-second personal commercial.

2. **Age groups.** When I became a sales representative at age twenty-two, I quickly joined the Young Professionals Network (YPN) in my town. I gained friends with shared interests, and I also built a strong network of future leaders. I highly recommend this group.

3. **Gender groups.** I attend Women in Business lunches through the chamber and also attend other events and organizations for professional women. It's important to

build a diverse network. Sharing common ground, as women, always gets the conversation going.

4. **Business journal events.** This could include industry-specific events, award ceremonies, and so on. Many business journals have "40 under 40" events, celebrations for the best places to work, and other such events. These all include movers and shakers. Even if it's not your industry, attend.

5. **Trade/professional association membership.** I not only participated in our trade association's meetings, but I also sat on the board. This gave me the valuable opportunity to build strong relationships with prospective clients and show them my commitment to the community and the industry. This was very successful and produced a huge return on my time. When I went from a sales role to owning a company, I had to cut back my networking events (but please note that this was after four years of networking almost every night), so I left the board when my term ended, but I still return to attend association events regularly, and if I am unavailable, I send a colleague. I always make sure to attend big association events. You should too! You're never too well known to stop networking.

6. **Charities.** At the start of my career, I joined a few charity organizations. I gained strong relationships with the committee members because we would meet regularly each month. I took it seriously. I learned how meetings were run and how others participated. This helped me facilitate my own meetings later on, but it also made it possible to show

them my work ethic and commitment to the charity by always being on time, participating, and sharing my ideas.

7. **Trade shows.** Industry-specific trade shows are excellent places to get acquainted, get sales, and get ahead. Not in a sales role? That's okay! This is one of the best venues to meet potential clients and like-minded individuals and to learn from your competition.

The Smartt Meeting Method

Since every meeting is an investment of time, I go in with a clear set of objectives. I'm there to network and make connections. Here's how:

1. I have quick conversations with as many people as I can, **and I get at least one really unique thing from them that I record on the back of the business card they hand me.**

2. Later, I'm able to follow up with them on that **one thing**. For example, if John mentions something to me about his two dogs, I write down their names, Einstein and Mack. I make a note of something obviously unique to John so John understands I really heard **him** and I wasn't just moving on to the next person, and the next, and the next.

3. I e-mail John the next day and say, "Hey, John, it was great meeting you at the Petaluma Young Professional's Network last night. I hope Einstein and Mack are bearing up under the heat this week."

4. Then I suggest a way to make the acquaintanceship practical for both of us.

I try to build each of these contacts into personal relationships. To me, each of them really is very special.

Make a Note

Never be afraid to make notes to help build your connections with people. I write salient details (like the earlier dog example) on the back of business cards people hand me, and I do it pretty quickly. If people don't hand me a card, it's a little tricky. As soon as I'm done talking to them, I pull out my phone, and in my Notes app, I write their name (so that I don't forget it) and the unique detail, and then I search for the name on LinkedIn or Google in order to find his/her e-mail address.

Cards Count

Sometimes, surprisingly, I'll get an e-mail from these new people because I always give out my business cards, and they e-mail me first. I've found business cards to be invaluable, and I've seen the kinds of unfortunate repercussions for people who didn't have enough of them or left them at home. Always bring your business cards. You are in business, after all, and they are an inexpensive way to make an impression.

New Friends

Seek these five top qualities in the friends you choose and you can't go wrong:

1. Ambition

2. Integrity

3. Loyalty

4. Honesty

5. Compassion

Small Talk

How do you make a networking event work for you? It's not rocket science. Just start off with a few basic questions:

- What's your name?
- What do you do? Where do you work?
- What brings you here?

The last question is a good way to discover the other person's passions and interests. And if that person says, "free shrimp!"—well, at least you know.

If I can get all that personal information in one encounter, then I have enough information to research those individuals at a later date and know what they might need from me and how I can help them. Hopefully, by that time, I've impressed them by asking them about themselves. Remember that people love to talk about themselves. The point of networking is to get to know other people. By asking them questions, you're showing that you care. People love this.

Keep your goals in mind when you attend a networking event. Connect with people. Gather information. Connect them with other people. Be remembered. Perhaps you'll make an easy connection in two seconds. If so, those two seconds have earned you trust. How quick is that? One of the easiest ways to gain people's loyalty is to connect them to people they need to know.

Smartt Steps

Five things you should know about everyone within ten minutes of saying hello:

1. What they do. You'll know more than just their job title after a ten-minute conversation. That should give you a good read on whether or not you can be useful to each other in the future.

2. Their name. Really, the introduction is the most important; first impressions really do matter. Repeat their name to make sure you have it right immediately after they introduce themselves.

3. Their passions. Structure your conversations such that you get an understanding of what people are most passionate about. Ask lots of questions, and listen attentively to their answers.

4. How you can be of help. Based on what they do and what they're passionate about, you should have some understanding of how you can be useful to them. It might be a collaboration, it might be connecting them with someone in your field who would be a great resource, or it might be a job tip. Ten minutes is plenty of time to make sense of how to leverage this kind of networking connection.

5. How to follow up. Find out their preferred method of contact, and make sure to exchange information.

"We don't have a choice on whether we do social media, the question is how well we do it."

ERIK QUALMAN

STEP SIX

Become a Master of Social Media

When I first meet people, I think about *how* I'm going to connect with them. As a rule, I always connect first through LinkedIn, the professionals' network. If they become instant connections, I may add them to my Facebook page, which serves as a platform for some clients and new friends. People want to build relationships with people they know, like, trust, and with whom a clear, visible connection has been made.

I've learned a lot about how best to use social media and where to spend the most time to effectively build my business and network. The social media swamp is wide and deep, and you can lose a lifetime of hours in it. So take a break, back away from the monitor, and give some thought to how to use social media the way professional people use it: not for play but for work.

Social media is ubiquitous, but it also provides a host of new and emerging ways to connect, gather information, stay transparent, and remain informed—and what goes for personal relationships goes for business relationships too. Social media can help you make great strides in your career and help immensely if you're just starting out.

Eight Social Platforms (in Order of Importance) That Can Have an Impact on Your Career

Here are the eight social platforms you need to be using, in order of importance.

1. **LinkedIn.** If you're in a professional career, then this should go without saying. You must be on LinkedIn. Recruiters use the platform to find great talent. You can easily build a strong network and become known as a leader in your industry. LinkedIn has a ton to offer. You can join groups, find other people your contacts already know, discover connections between people and interests, read informative articles, stay up-to-date on changes in your industry or at specific companies, and so on. Make sure to use LinkedIn to your best advantage.

2. **Facebook.** This highest-ranking social media site is still viewed mostly for personal use, but many businesses promote their products and services here too. I use it for staying up to date with connections and sharing great advice and some personal photos. I visit regularly to stay on top of personal events and news. I have added some clients to my Facebook page because I am a firm believer that sharing some personal details makes relationships stronger—but I have nothing on my Facebook page that I wouldn't want my parents to see. (Remember, party pictures, while they may be cool, shouldn't be posted on any social media platform, no matter how private your settings. Keep the photos professional.)

3.   **Twitter.** Don't overlook this platform if you're looking to connect with people nationally and grow a broader demographic for your network. I've met very influential people through Twitter, people who have secured speaking gigs for me, given me information about conferences I never would have known about, and helped me make many more unique connections. In fact, it's through Twitter that I learned about Inc. magazine's list of the top five thousand fastest-growing companies. I submitted Star Staffing for it, and we came in 2690 out of 5000. Join Twitter chats to engage with your followers, create valuable content, and create lists for people to follow. Want to know my favorite Twitter chats? Follow me @Nicole_Smartt and ask!

4.   **Instagram.** This is a growing platform that I use for posting motivational quotes, as well as news about business meetings, awards, get-togethers with friends, and personal stuff. It's important to connect with your audience and show that you are not just all work, so share your personality, your progress, and things about your actual life. Use it to show people a snapshot of who you really are.

5.   **WordPress.** I use WordPress to post my blogs on my website and provide great content. Through this platform, I am able to easily customize the look and feel of my site, which helps manage my brand. Having content readily available that demonstrates your strengths and positions you as an authority in your field is essential in today's world. It can also be a great, reflective exercise to write and post content and share your perspective on other people's articles. It doesn't take a ton of time, and WordPress can **do** practically

anything, yet it doesn't take a computer science degree to get started. You can just blog and go.

6. **YouTube.** I've created only a few videos, but I know this is one area I need to develop. Videos are increasingly used in the business world to get concepts, sales pitches, new product launches—practically everything—into the hands of the people who need to know. The video format is flexible and easy, and you don't need big, fancy setups anymore. It takes a little bit of getting used to, but once you've got your personal style nailed down, you can make and post a video in about fifteen minutes. YouTube is free, ubiquitous, and highly searchable.

7. **Pinterest.** While I enjoy Pinterest for personal use, including shopping and creating vision boards, I utilize it more for posting content and sharing my blogs. Pinterest has a high return on Google for searchable items, and it gets content out there. You may find in your particular environment that Pinterest is far more useful to you and comes in closer to the top than #7. And who knows? It may become more useful to me, businesswise, in the future.

8. **Snapchat.** I use this to connect with others every day. Snapchat is super low overhead, fun, and helps me stay connected with the people I care about most, even on a really busy schedule.

There are others, of course. Google+, for example, is great for search engine optimization (SEO) since, obviously, it's connected to Google. If you post there, you get a higher ranking in Google, so I do recommend linking your blogs and articles to the network.

Google has announced that they will be making significant changes to Google+, so it's best to use it mainly for distribution rather than creating and storing content.

My Top Three Social Media Don'ts

Avoid these things on social media (almost) always:

1. **Whining—of any kind.** If you feel the urge to whine, ask a question instead. Don't use social media to vent frustrations or to be negative—unless your airline loses your luggage, and it is never found, and social media is the only way to get their attention.

2. **Neurosis.** In concert with whining, avoid passive aggression. If you're upset with someone, take it offline. If you put that stuff on social media, you've made your reputation Swiss cheese. When people make negative comments anywhere on social media, you can remove those people from your lists of social media contacts, or you can respond in a polite manner. It's your call. (Again, why associate yourself with negative people?)

3. **Evidence.** That thing about keeping crazy party pictures offline? Take it seriously. I went to Miami to see the Golden State Warriors play the Miami Heat. After the game, my friends and I went out to some fun and happening spots. At one of those places, a photographer asked for my name. I gave it to him, not thinking. The photographer tagged my name in photos, and I had a tough time getting them taken down. Be careful. You can still have fun, but keep it off the Internet as best as you can.

Let's Chat SEO

Search Engine Optimization (SEO) is essential to getting you the online followers you're looking for and making sure you're branded correctly. SEO is the process of making sure that a search engine (such as Google or Yahoo) understands what your web pages contain and thus can display your pages in unpaid (commonly called "organic") search engine results.

I recommend taking free classes on SEO. I found some by Googling SEO best practices. You can also go to Google's website and review their principles. Many online webinars are free, and I would start there. If you have questions about my favorite webinars, shoot me an e-mail at Nicole@NicoleSmartt.com.

Have You Googled Your Name?

If not, I advise you to stop reading and do so now. Do you rank first on the page? Awesome! Do you have to scroll to the third page to find your entry? Time for work! When you start to build your network and your brand, people will begin searching for you on the Internet, and you want to come up first. This takes work, but by blogging regularly, actively working social media, gaining press mentions, and guest posting on other people's blogs—among many other options—you can get your name onto the first page. The rule of thumb is simple: the more often your name is used on web pages, the more often it will turn up in searches. And the more often it turns up in searches, the more likely it is you will turn up at the top of the Google search. (Although, if your name is, say, Katy Perry, finding you and not the singer will be a real nightmare!)

Every Network Has a Purpose

Use each platform to post different types of information. For instance, Twitter posts scroll down in real time, whereas an Instagram post from a week ago or a year ago may still be viewable. Facebook has two different views in its newsfeed: top stories and most recent. So unsponsored content might never be seen. LinkedIn is a little bit more linear, but it is not quite as predictable as Facebook.

You.com

Own yourself on the web. It's not about vanity. It's about building your brand. Google is indispensable, so you want to make sure people who are looking for you can find you. The best way to make sure that happens is to use your own name as your URL. Instead of "random-idea.com," go to a web registrar such as GoDaddy.com or dotster.com, and claim "your-own-real-name.com." Register it and keep it. You can always build a website later. Even if you don't have a business or don't plan to, it's important that you own your name on the web. For example, I own NicoleSmartt.com. It's important to do this because you don't want someone else buying it up. It's your name, after all! The costs of owning your own URL are minimal, and the returns are extraordinary.

LinkedIn: a Labor of (Marketing) Love

I try to devote an hour every day to LinkedIn. That sounds like a lot of time to block off for social media, but you'll actually be surprised at what you'll get in return.

Whether you're a job seeker or a recruiter, a sales representative or a CEO, an assembler or a lawyer, having a top-viewed LinkedIn profile can be a big benefit to your career. As a top 1 percent LinkedIn member with 6,118 (and counting) connections, I've found that this position leads to a number of great things: an expanded network, more exposure, and new business. In fact, customers often call and say they found me on LinkedIn. They read the articles I publish and promote on LinkedIn, or they learn about our Star brand and want to do business with a respected leader.

LinkedIn also does a couple of things better than any other platform out there right now: it connects professionals in a more useful way, and it connects them more easily to new networks. Endorsements, easily digestible descriptions of work done for clients, integrated resumes, and work examples all make LinkedIn an unparalleled tool for making great connections.

Most importantly, since I started dedicating an hour a day to LinkedIn (even on weekends), I've had a high return on investment with job seekers reaching out to me, new clients wanting to do business, networks offering speaking opportunities, media outlets offering writing gigs, and my company's own brand becoming better known. All these things equal money and exposure for me and for the company, at no cost. I'm not telling you these things to plug LinkedIn for its own sake. I'm telling you because this strategy has helped me, and it can help you. Here are my favorite strategies for getting greater exposure on LinkedIn:

1. **Start blogging.** With LinkedIn's Pulse, you're able to post as many articles as you want. Writing expert content related to your business or role will increase your exposure, gain you followers, and help you be viewed as an expert. If you're not yet an expert, research and become an expert on something. If you're searching for work, write articles on what you look for in a company and why. All of these factors will help show others why you'd make a valuable addition to their

network. It can also open up more opportunities for you than just a sale or a job.

2. **Share, share, and share some more—but be strategic.** Share content with friends and link to it in your e-mail signature. Send articles to your connections letting them know that you're thinking of them. The key is to be strategic and to know when to check in with connections with something genuinely helpful, interesting, and relevant. I share one post a day on my status update as well as a few articles in different groups to attract a larger audience. I also share articles with friends and acquaintances if the content is appropriate and relevant. You have to be selective and strategic. It's a busy world, and not everyone wants to be bombarded by your blog or shared articles, so make it worthwhile. For example, if there's a new law in your industry, share it. If it's a cute picture of a kitten and you have a friend who is kitty obsessed, send it in a message. Think about who would really benefit from this content, and then share it with that person.

3. **Connect and build.** One way to build your network is to add to it frequently. Network with groups. Look to see who is sharing content and using LinkedIn consistently. Connect with those people first. If you meet people in real life who could be good professional connections, search for them on LinkedIn and interact with them there. Every time I connect with people, I send them an introductory e-mail. This is not the same as making a sales pitch. If you are a sales professional, you should not send messages about your service/product. You'll get a quick delete. My introductory

message goes something like this: "Hi Joe! Nice to e-meet you. I appreciate your connecting with me. If there is anything I can do to assist you, please don't hesitate to ask. I can also be found on Twitter @Nicole_Smartt. If you're on Twitter, follow me and I'll follow back. All the best, Nicole Smartt." Direct, simple, and with no sales pitch. It works. Try it for a month and see where it gets you.

4. **Engage once a day if you're job hunting.** This will keep you top of mind. It's also important to post relevant information to show you're a reputable individual with a solid work ethic. For instance, if you're looking for a position in human resources, write an article about why you got your original degree in marketing but how you'd now like to start in HR. Connect with groups, and follow companies of interest.

5. **Use the LinkedIn Connect app.** This will help you stay in the know for anniversaries, birthdays, job opportunities, events, and so much more. This is my go-to app. It will update you and give you everything you need to stay connected. Use it daily.

It takes time, but how you spend that time can add up to a large return on investment. Trust me. LinkedIn brought me several clients, and one of them was my biggest client. I never pitched those clients, and I didn't spend money on sales advertisements. I simply used my time wisely on LinkedIn. Invest in yourself, and invest in your connections. Remember, I'm always happy to connect. You should be too.

Go Guru

Use LinkedIn to position yourself as an expert or a thought leader in your field. Whether you're an expert on how things are now or on the leading edge of brand-new ways to do things in your industry, **show it**. Expertise is a strange and partially manufactured thing, but being really good at what you do will shine. You can position yourself as a guru by posting or linking to other articles you've written or reports you can take some credit for that show people you know your stuff.

Content Is Queen

Focus on delivering valuable content on every platform, and your followers and relationships will blossom.

Blog and Then Blog Some More

LinkedIn has a platform called Pulse, which is LinkedIn's blogging site. If you don't have a blogging site, use Pulse. Your posts will be sent to your entire network. Pulse is its own network, and people can view it by category. If you have your own blog, link to it through categories so people with an interest in your topic will find your posts. Other publications might pick up articles this way as well. For example, Pulse could pick your post up, and you could be Pulse's "Highlight of the Week." That gets your post sent out to Pulse's entire network, which is everybody on LinkedIn because it's a LinkedIn product. With LinkedIn, your potential reach is huge.

My second tip is to blog in WordPress. The WordPress content tool is really easy to use. You can create your own WordPress account in a few minutes and start blogging from there. If you want to get a little bit higher scale, you could create your own website and then use WordPress as a content-management tool, but you'll have to buy a domain name to do that.

Smartt Steps

1. Do a social media self-assessment. Are your profiles up to date? Are they professional? Are you happy with the way you appear there?

2. Google yourself. Evaluate what comes up. Then plan an "upgrade" of your search results. Blogging, LinkedIn articles, and reworking keywords on existing content can all help.

3. Build plans to share social media content strategically. Ask yourself: what are you trying to get out of this share? What do you want people to do?

4. Build a blog plan. Write ahead, and schedule posts.

5. Use the LinkedIn Connect app. It really cuts down on time and effort.

> *"Leadership is about making others better as a result of your presence and making sure that impact lasts in your absence."*
> SHERYL SANDBERG

STEP SEVEN

Lead by Example

I spent a lot of my childhood on teams, surrounded by people who wanted the same thing I wanted: a win! So it's not surprising I learned leadership from teammates, from challenges and effort, and especially from my basketball coaches. From an early age, I was surrounded by strong leaders.

Strong leaders are those who lead by example. They walk the talk, and as a result, they become people others want to follow. By consistently displaying leadership traits, they generate trust, credibility, and authority. These traits are essential to the development of a strong leader.

Five Great Leadership Traits

1. **Be there, and be prepared.** Leaders need to be positive, supportive, and informative. When I played basketball, the coaches were our leaders; they were always there before us. They were always prepared. They spoke to each team member, and if someone wasn't performing well, they

spent extra time training and mentoring that person. They led us to victory.

2. **Provide solutions.** Always. No one wants to hear you whine. Whining hasn't done any good for anyone who seeks to lead others. In order to stand out as a leader, you need to be solutions oriented. That means seeing a challenge and coming up with solutions to solve it. When I faced a challenge in business, I would approach my manager with the challenge and a handful of my solutions. This allowed her the option of choosing the one she thought best. She looked at me as a leader because I was able to provide solutions to problems. Don't dwell on problems; instead, be the first to offer solutions.

3. **Listen. Ask questions. Seek to understand.** Great leaders are excellent listeners. When they speak, they do so clearly, confidently, and without hesitation. This one was tough for me as I always thought the loudest person in the room was the smartest or most powerful, when in fact it was usually the quiet person who asked questions and listened to the answers. You will receive valuable insights and set a tone that encourages healthy dialogue if you learn to listen. When you ask questions, listen with complete attention. When you're done with the conversation, write a short note summarizing it. You'll feel more informed later and have a record in case you forget details.

4. **Demonstrate emotional intelligence.** Emotional intelligence is an essential part of being a good leader. Those who have emotional intelligence have the capacity to recognize their own emotions and those of others, and use that information

to guide their thinking and behavior. Being able to use emotional intelligence to avoid volatile eruptions in order to produce a rational, fact-based, data-driven strategy is the mark of a great leader. Weak leaders shout. Strong leaders listen and ask questions. Using restraint to guide your thinking and decisions makes you a powerful communicator and advocate.

5. **Lead with honesty and integrity.** It's as simple as this: if you let your integrity slip or you're dishonest with your team, you'll lose credibility and your ability to lead effectively will weaken. The converse is also true: if your team sees you bringing high standards to the table, they'll try to help you succeed. Strong leaders raise the bar for all and help all members of the team achieve success. That's what honesty, integrity, and hard work can do.

True influence and confident leadership don't happen overnight. They are a combination of the previous five traits plus a whole lot of time, effort, and sustained concentration. Influencers stand out in their field and are personable and generous; their excitement is often infectious (even if they're quiet people).

Respecting Winners, Supporting Others

One of many traits that makes someone a great leader is being able to acknowledge excellence without diminishing anyone else in the process. **A great business team never plays a zero-sum game.**

Leadership Means Taking Responsibility

As a leader, you have to learn to accept responsibility wisely and take it when you need to. You might not always be in the right, and when you're not, you need to be able to say, "I'm sorry. I was wrong. You were right." Everybody is wrong from time to time. "I was wrong" are three of the most powerful words a leader can speak. Leaders unable to say those three words are destined to fail. Taking responsibility is what leadership is all about. It opens the door to finding solutions. When you accept responsibility, you're signaling to your team that despite setbacks, you're ready to look for the right answer.

Failure

The very word suggests loss and defeat. But it's not that at all. It's a way of examining experiences and finding ways of turning them from negatives to positives. It's okay to fail if you've failed while trying your best. That's how we learn and grow. You are not going to win every game. You are not going to close every business deal. Nobody's perfect, and owning that is important. Being aware of your own pitfalls and sticking points can help too.

Responsibility Is Something You Should Try to Own

I'm a leader. That means I need to be aware of how I lead my team during moments of conflict and challenge. If we are losing a client, for example, I get upset and must avoid projecting that energy onto others. I need to ignore blame altogether until the crisis has passed and focus instead on damage control. Calling people out on their mistakes, especially in public, is a waste of time and can sap a team of the positive energy that's needed to repair the problem. First, focus on solutions and repair. When you're out of the weeds, you can think about how it happened and put measures in place to prevent future mistakes. Using the "5 Whys" is a great way to discover answers without placing blame on one person. Start with the problem:

"We lost a client." Then ask, "Why?" Answer: "We didn't address a concern they raised." Why? "We're too busy." And so on. The crux of the problem could very well be a process failure that you can fix.

Here are some top lessons I learned from my coaches and a few of my teammates related to being a good leader:

- **Lead by example.** You can't lead until you can become a person others want to follow. When leaders say one thing but do another, they erode trust, a critical element of productive leadership.

- **Handle conflicts proactively.** Proactive conflict resolution takes grace, and works differently for each person but you'll find your version. Disagreements are bound to happen, but the final snapshot is very, very different when a disagreement is allowed to devolve into a shouting match rather than a gentle reminder that everyone is entitled to an opinion. Shouting is not productive for anyone. If your habit of listening and asking questions has spread to your team, you'll have an easier time with this.

- **Show trust and good faith.** Expect sound reasoning, even from people who disagree on big issues, and listen to alternative solutions. You'll cultivate a calmer, more productive, more cohesive team, and you'll solve big problems better and faster if you assume you are on the same side and want the same things.

- **Establish standards.** Set standards and then hold yourself to them. If you establish standards of accountability, transparency, and problem solving, and then model the behavior you're expecting from others accordingly, you'll guide your team to behave in the same way. From a leadership position, this is an excellent method of setting expectations and getting your whole team aligned while remaining graceful, team oriented, and collaborative.

- **Prove you're a positive leader.** If you want to be in charge, be in charge of what you can control. If you're trying to move into a leadership role, you need to take on any assignment that you're given and aim higher for the job that you want. Take the next task that comes along and demonstrate that you can do it. You need to demonstrate that you're someone who can be counted on.

- **Empathize.** Managers lead in two ways: by fear—screaming, "You're fired!"—or **by showing others what winning looks like. Everyone will choose victory over fear.** So not only do you need to aim higher, but you also need to empathize with your coworkers, at every level. A lot of leaders have empathy as one of their strengths, but be aware that *empathy* isn't the same as *sympathy*. Empathy happens on an even playing field, peer to peer. Sympathy is hierarchic. Bringing your empathy into the office helps you read how team members are feeling about their workload and whether or not they feel supported. It makes seeing situations from multiple perspectives easier, and it makes you a positive problem solver.

Follow Your Mentors' Good Examples

I've learned a lot from my mentors over the years. I learned the value and importance of hard work from my dad who worked six days a week, and I learned what it takes to run a successful business from Nadine and Carl. As I mentioned earlier, mentors are everywhere; you just have to take notice. I find mentors online who are thought leaders in certain areas and gain expertise and knowledge from them. Remember, these are real people, and they had help getting where they are today. Don't be afraid to ask them questions. Engage with them. Learn from them. They are clearly doing something right.

Watch and Read

Much of what I have learned about leadership has come from watching others and reading leadership books. As a result of my observations and research, I knew I wanted to be a leader with high standards, someone who was intent on making things better than they were the day before. I also knew that I would need to cultivate a team of high achievers in order to meet those standards. So I took what I had learned from my mentors, and I developed goals for myself that would help me become a respected leader in my own right.

Encourage Team Spirit

I made it a goal to encourage team spirit and collaboration from the beginning. I've always felt that managers who aren't willing to get their hands dirty to get things done aren't really effective managers in the long run. If you aren't down in the trenches with your crew, how can you really understand what it's like to be them? How can you understand their struggles and their successes? Relying only on what they report to you breeds confusion for a whole host of reasons. It's better to keep yourself in touch with what it's like to be everyone from the janitor to the CEO. You'll become a more compassionate and effective leader as a result.

Stay in Touch

Have you ever seen *Undercover Boss*? The premise of the show is that somebody from upper management goes in disguise to a position on the bottom rung to see what life is really like in the trenches. From an owner's perspective, I can understand why many CEOs failed at the entry-level positions: consultants are constantly telling CEOs to work *on* their business and not *in* it. But that's ludicrous and here's why. If we aren't working *in* our business, how do we know what to work *on*? This is my philosophy. Yes, some of the companies on *Undercover Boss* were vast enterprises with many hidden corners. But a bit of time in a starting position can help a CEO stay in touch with customers, employees, and the company's vision and mission.

Finding a Good Mentor

When we're young, people tell us what to do, what to wear, what not to wear, and what not to do. As we grow, we learn to fend for ourselves and to each become our own person, choosing what we want to do and what we want to wear. When we get into our careers and get stuck, we reach out to a business coach or consultant for help—I am always seeking to learn and collaborate—but we must take care to select the right mentors. Are their goals aligned with ours? Are they where we want to be in life? Have they done what we've done, but better? Many people want to work for themselves, so they decide to become a consultant. This is very different from being a consultant who ran a multimillion-dollar company and is now retired and consulting for fun.

Three Practical Ways to Commit to Excellence

Committing to excellence is the hallmark of a leader. Here are three ways to lead a pack:

1.   **Look ahead with confidence.** It doesn't matter where you're directing your efforts. If you're committed to excellence, it will show in your outcomes.

2. **Don't settle for less.** Settling for less than your best doesn't gain you anything except a mounting sense of dissatisfaction. When you don't settle, you're insisting on something better.

3. **Model yourself after people you respect and who have achieved excellence.** They are living testaments to success.

Bonus tip: if you have the chance, ask people you respect what they attribute their success to.

Smartt Steps

1. Exercise caution in choosing the right mentors.

2. Practice being impeccable with your word.

"Some people want it to happen, some people wish it would happen, others make it happen."
MICHAEL JORDAN

STEP EIGHT

Hustle, Always Hustle

This chapter exists to help you understand the value of hustling. It always comes down to work ethic and performance. When I accepted the promotion to the position of sales representative from that of recruiter, I researched and found I had some serious competition! One competitor had been successful for over seven years, dominating the marketplace and representing a local company with a great reputation. I didn't let this deter me or get me down. There is no time for self-pity. It is an absolute waste of time.

Control Your Own Destiny

I needed to figure out how I could outperform, outwork, and outhustle my competition because what it comes down to is hustle. You can outperform the smartest person, you can outperform the richest person, and you can outperform the current best in the game. So that's what I did.

In order to outsell my competition, I made sure to attend three networking events a week and cold-call twenty-five businesses each day. Remember, at this time, social media wasn't the craze it is today. Throughout that two-year process, I learned a whole lot about approaching people, about providing a better experience than my competition, and about ultimately winning customers.

After five years of constant networking, I learned many of the skills that prepared me to own my own business. All of that hard work and determination was finally paying off, and I was one step closer to living my dream of owning my own business.

If you're ambitious and ready to hustle to achieve your own dreams, here are a few steps to get you started.

Know Your Competition

It comes down to research and homework. Most of your direct competitors aren't going to meet you for lunch and cough up their methods or their secret approaches to success. But you can learn a whole lot about salespeople from the trail they leave on—that's right—the Internet.

Here's another way LinkedIn can be incredibly useful. Let's say you're trying to get a read on your competition (in any particular area, though my examples will come from a sales perspective). On LinkedIn, you can look through a competitor's connections, posts, and work history. You may even be able to determine who their current clients are, and from their business website, you may be able to reverse-engineer their methods.

Don't be afraid to look them up as individuals too. You can learn a *lot* from an individual's online presence, including things such as their attitude in general, how much and how far they travel (for work, of course), their intelligence, whether or not they have followers, and so on. Approach this research as if you were considering hiring them, or to really zero in, research them as if you were considering working under them.

But what if I can't find anything useful about them online? Good question. You can still cold-call; you can still learn tons from their current or former clients or customers. There are a myriad of angles to try.

Do What They Do, but Better

Try the methods they're using. Learn from their mistakes as well as their successes! The more you understand about your competition, the larger your repository of experience. Once you have an understanding of what your competition is doing well and not so well, consider ways to improve their process.

1. Can you make it faster?

2. Can you make it more effective?

3. Can you scale it so you're doing more work in the same amount of time (or less)?

For the areas where your competition isn't excelling, ask yourself these questions:

- Are they underperforming because of the industry they're in, the economic landscape of their industry, or some force that is completely beyond their control? If not . . .
- Is laziness at play? If so, don't be lazy. Put in effort where others don't and you're nearly guaranteed to pull ahead.
- If there is a particular pain point that salespeople seem to be missing or failing to address for their prospective (or existing) clientele, why are they not addressing it? Is it a difficult problem to solve?

Allow yourself to continue growing in the position, but set an aggressive growth timeline. Adopt the easiest-to-implement methods you learned from your competition and then weigh the value of the remaining methods. Lay groundwork and then build.

The Hustle Begins and Ends with You

Even in situations where you're pushed by aggressive sales goals, demanding bosses, or in other pressing situations, ultimately, the hustle begins and ends with what you bring to the table—what you're willing to do. You know your limits. Be willing to stretch them and surprise yourself. The willingness to push ahead, to try new things, to make those extra few calls or connections every day is where you pull ahead. That's where you outperform. I'm not suggesting you sacrifice everything else in your life for the hustle, but if there's fat in your days that you can trim, trim it.

Discipline Is a Direct Link to Success

It's not just important to make lists. It's more important to complete the items on that list. Discipline is a funny thing. We all have days when it seems insurmountable to even *start* a task from our to-do list or to even write a list. But here is where you have a chance to prove to yourself that you can succeed: *do it anyway*. Discipline gives you a leg up on the tepid competition all the way up to the top. So set goals for yourself (twenty-five connections a day, whether through cold calls or Internet introductions, for instance), and then complete them. Don't leave any for tomorrow. The calls cascade if you let them— don't let this happen. *Make the last two calls.*

Get It Done

When you're looking at a mountain of work, fractionalize it. Take one task at a time, and bring your best to it. When you're finished and ready to move on to the next thing, you'll know you've done it all well.

Practice Makes Perfect

This is true of discipline, of adopting new work methods, of nailing down your elevator pitch, and of everything: just keep practicing. Evaluate often, and tweak your trajectory as you go. As in sales, so in life: the landscape is always changing, even in small ways. Responding instead of reacting makes you adaptable, lithe, and ultimately better at whatever it is you're doing. So go ahead and do that pitch in the mirror, and then a couple of weeks later, think about what you've learned in between, and see if changes based on this new information could make your pitch tighter, better.

Let Technology Help

There are tons and tons of "productivity" apps out there, all kinds of tools to help you stay organized and get ahead. Increasingly, companies have some sort of task management system in place, but even if they don't, there are many options. There are free and paid versions of many of those apps. If you need a simple task list, solutions such as Evernote and Google Tasks, in concert with the Google calendar, can be of tremendous help. They sync between devices, so if you think of something on your way into work, you can open the app and add a task, and it will show up on your other devices.

If you need to organize visually and by project, check out options such as Trello. You can see overviews in card form, and drill down on the details. If you need a little more structure (or to collaborate with coworkers) in a task-based environment, try something like Asana or

Basecamp. Poke around, see what you think might work for you, and adopt these tools. Don't be afraid to try several different methods to find one that works well with the way you think and how you use technology. It's a good bet that something out there can help.

Four Profiles in Perseverance

J. K. Rowling

After divorcing her husband, Rowling moved with her baby daughter to Edinburgh, Scotland, to be closer to her sister. It was there she began to write the first Harry Potter novel. She grew increasingly poor and struggled to support herself and her daughter, living on welfare. The first three chapters of her Harry Potter book were rejected by twelve publishing houses. It took a year of rejections before she was finally signed up and given an advance of £1,500 (about $2,250). The Harry Potter brand has grown and is now worth an estimated $15 billion.

Fred Smith

The FedEx founder first created his business model for an overnight delivery service for his college thesis. He turned it in and was given a bad grade for his efforts. After graduating in 1966, Smith went to war in Vietnam where he survived an ambush attack. When he returned in 1970, he went back to the idea in his college thesis and founded FedEx in 1971. His hardships didn't end there. After raising $91 million in venture capital, he turned around and lost $29 million of it, which almost cost him the business. Not knowing what to do, he went to Las Vegas and managed to win $27,000, saving his company.

Walt Disney

Walt Disney was originally fired from a Missouri newspaper for not being creative enough. He moved to Kansas City, where he opened a small company, Laugh-o-gram, which eventually went bankrupt. He and his brother, Roy, moved to Hollywood, where they opened a cartoon studio. The studio started to make successful cartoons, but despite launching Mickey and his Silly Symphony series, Disney again almost ran out of money before risking $1.5 million to develop the first full-length animated feature film, *Snow White and the Seven Dwarfs*, in 1937. The film has since made more than $400 million.

Steven Spielberg

Spielberg was rejected from the film school of the University of Southern California (USC) three times for having a C average before attending The California State University (CSU) in Long Beach, where he majored in English. While a student at CSU, he was offered an unpaid internship with Universal Studios. That internship turned into a seven-year directing contract, making him the youngest director to be signed on to a long-term directing deal with a major Hollywood studio. He promptly dropped out of college to pursue a career in directing with Universal Studios. He's now worth an estimated $3 billion and has donated a fortune to the USC film school.

Strive for Excellence, Always

Mediocre salespeople still get sales. But why are you going to show up if your goal isn't excellence? If your process can be improved, improve it. Look back at your competition and measure your landscape against what you can see of theirs.

It's not all about looking at your competition, though. You can always do better at whatever you're doing; there's no cap on excellence. Keep refining your hustle, keep asking harder questions, keep your discipline high, and don't let the inevitable setback get you down—or, at least, not for very long.

Head High, Keep Moving

There will be days when every (or almost every) call you make is a dead end and times when a new pitch you just put together flops spectacularly and leaves your conversation partner more confused than on board. That's okay. That's how we learn. Keep believing you can do it. Dissect what went wrong. For instance, if a pitch falls flat, don't worry that you've lost your hustle. Consider your prospective client: what's that person's industry, pain points, highest needs, problems that your service/product could solve? Did your pitch address those issues, or did you miss them?

Every experience is a learning experience. Tomorrow is always another day.

Three Ways to Step up Your Game

If you want to learn to hustle, it's as simple as one, two, three.

1. **Reach your own goals.** If you're competing against your last success, then you have pretty good control over your inner environment, and you're focusing your energy on improving your work instead of stressing about how you compare to others.

2. **Use others' performances to improve your own.** Keep your eye on what's working for others, and try out their

methods. Can't figure out how someone achieved a particularly effective outcome? Ask that person!

3. **Benchmark your progress.** When you set your own goals, design benchmarks to help you feel achievement during larger projects. Benchmarks help to keep you motivated!

Smartt Steps

1. Research events in your area that are relevant to you.

    - Make a list, including date and the cost to attend, if any.
    - Populate a calendar, and total up the cost for attendance in monthly chunks.
    - Work attendance at these functions into your regular schedule.

2. Prepare "sprints" of daunting tasks like sales calls. Have your lists prepared in advance.

3. Hold yourself accountable.

    - Keep a journal where you give yourself a grade every day. However you structure the grading scale, make it relevant to you. Use this data to understand how well you're planning.

"Your smile is your logo, your personality is your business card, how you leave others feeling after an experience with you becomes your trademark."

JAY DANZIE

STEP NINE

Remain True to Yourself: Embrace Authenticity

What are core values? Core values are the building blocks of how we see the world. For example, for me, an important core value is integrity. Honesty and strong moral principles are at the core of who I am. Core values inform every decision I make!

The Core Values Checklist

1. Is what I'm about to say in line with my core values?

2. Is it smart?

3. Is it truthful?

4. Is it kind?

5. Is it helpful?

A True Story about Core Values in Action

When I left the staffing firm to start my own company, I left for a few reasons. I had experience in every function of a staffing firm's operations, and I believed strongly that I could run my own company. I had a supportive network of people who trusted me, and perhaps most importantly, the company I was with no longer aligned with my vision or my values. The company was set on developing a new client every week instead of building relationships with the clients I had spent countless dollars to attract and countless hours to win. I increasingly felt that my commitment to providing stellar service to our customers, which was part of what made them loyal in the first place, was less important to the company than sheer numbers. It didn't make sense to me, so I worked up the courage to start my own business.

That sounds as if the decision was easy to make. It wasn't. But, ultimately, I needed to stay true to my own core values, and that's what really sealed the new trajectory for me. I had to stay on my own inner course, and that just wasn't possible at that company. Knowing what you want and working toward it is essential—on the job and outside the office. Your perfectly aligned life will never just fall into your lap; it's handcrafted in pieces, discovered in napkin doodles and in conversations with friends on the phone. It takes work to stay on course, but you'll feel it if you start to waver. That strange dissatisfaction that comes from working in a position or for a company that just doesn't sit right with your inner compass is unmistakable.

Use Core Values as Your Compass

How do you detect an organization's core values? Find the "team" page on their website and dig around for key words and phrases that resonate with you. Don't be afraid to look these people up on social media to see how well they are living up to their own values. It can be pretty obvious. Keep in mind that there are formalities for businesses to consider, and many different types of people look at the "About Us" pages, so you might have to take implied meanings at face value. Then go back and look at the job description for the position you're interested in. Does it seem to align with the company's values, or is it "corporate speak"? If it's unclear, don't let that deter you. Many companies rely on corporate boilerplate. Once you find a company that seems to align well with your values, be prepared to ask questions in an interview. Remember, you and your interviewer are interviewing each other. You are not on trial.

Persistence Is a Good Value Too

If you aren't positive about what you want yet and haven't discovered your "big vision," that's okay! Keep digging, keep learning, and stay on the lookout for the signs that indicate a direction that would work well for you.

If you do know what you want, great! Set goals, and then break down into manageable chunks the steps you need to take to achieve those goals. Set tasks that move you toward your goal, however incrementally, and do a handful of them every day. However many you can manage is great. You're moving in the right direction.

Bring More Than Luck with You

Finding yourself in a role with an organization that matches or closely resembles your own values can happen by accident, but don't rely on serendipity to get you there. I've found that looking at a company's mission and vision statements can be helpful, but the best way I've been able to discern a company's real core values is by reviewing its mission and vision and then looking closely at the personal statements of the founders and the longest-standing employees.

My Top Five Core Values and Why They Are So Important to Me

1. **Integrity.** I must feel I am a person of integrity. I have a personal obligation to uphold the highest ethical standards and never compromise my values. I do what I say I am going to do and never make a promise I can't keep.

2. **Hard work.** I believe that working hard is an honest and honorable way to forward my career. And the proof of its success is seen in the results I achieve.

3. **Achievement.** I am constantly seeking new ideas and better ways to deliver results in all aspects of my life. I pursue excellence in everything I do, even in the smallest of tasks, because I have found that true excellence is achieved by doing many, many small things very well.

4. **Loyalty.** When I believe in a goal or a person, I dedicate myself to providing intelligent, useful support no matter what distractions and temptations may cross my path.

5. **Honesty.** It's last on this list, but first in overall importance. Honesty makes all things possible. Without it, there can be no trust or partnerships of value.

Some Notes about Setting Goals

There are many great resources already out there about setting and attaining goals, so I'm not going to go on about them here, but I do want to share a couple of things I've learned over the years about goal setting.

1. **Have a vision.** I was adamant that I was going to either start my own company or be a partner of a staffing firm by age thirty, and due to my hard work and determination, I was an owner by age twenty-five. Every day, anywhere I went, my goals were in sight. I put Post-it notes all through my house—on the fridge, on every mirror, at the office, in my car, and on my nightstand. Seeing my goals everywhere motivated me to constantly do things that would get me one step closer to making my dream a reality. Every year, I attend a vision party with friends. We bring a bunch of magazines and start cutting away to our vision-board masterpiece. It's important for you to know and see what you want to achieve.

2. **Break large goals into small tasks.** This will help you achieve your goals more quickly.

3. **Be realistic, and then be a little aggressive.** Once you have a goal in place, discrete tasks will begin to appear. Take the amount of effort (in time, in resources—wherever effort will be applied) that each task will require, and add up that effort in time if you can. Look at the other things (in your life or at work) that take up your time. Evaluate what you can let go of or put on hold to help you get to your goal faster, and then see what time you have left. Assign tasks

accordingly, but remember humans are living creatures, and sick days, setbacks, and surprises will happen. When you have good plans in place, it's much easier to account for and adjust to unknown factors, and ultimately stay on track after unexpected events occur.

Vision: Why It's Important

Without a vision, you cannot recognize success. So having a vision is essential to goal achievement. After all, if you haven't envisioned the ultimate goal, how will you know when you've arrived? Having a vision helps you arrive at success as *you* define it, on your terms. If you can't answer the dreaded question "Where do you see yourself in five years?" you're a whole lot more prone to ending up in a position, in work or in life, that doesn't resonate with the true you.

It should start with a vision and continue with goal setting that supports that vision. Then you should assign tasks (for yourself, coworkers—whoever's helping your vision become a reality), and define the steps you will take and the discipline you will employ to get there. Without a vision, you might find that a year or two down the road you've achieved all of these goals, but they don't line up with each other, or there are big gaps in the picture. Or you might find yourself with a ton of new customers initially, but because you don't have a process in place to sustain existing customers, at the end of three years, you had *less than what you started with.*

Know What You Can Live With

It's important when people are interviewing for a new position that they find out whether the core values of a new employer are compatible with theirs. That's job number one. They should learn what the company's vision is. Can they stand behind that vision and mission? Do they fit with those core values, or is that going to be a problem for them?

Stop! Look! Listen! And Reflect!

Life is a series of railroad crossings; you never know what's coming, so it always pays to pause and think before going on. Your thinking time doesn't have to be in complete solitude. You don't have to go into reflection as a monk does. Your thinking time could take place as you're driving. Some of my reflection time is spent trying to figure out what I could have done better. But other times it's just about getting away from work and focusing on something else. Or going to the gym. Or going to hang with my pet goats. So whether reflection happens because my goats take me out of my work drama, making me happy and making me laugh, or whether I find reflection during time with friends, it's important to not let the day-to-day negativity impact your life.

Take Shelter

Make sure you have some kind of safe haven, a place where you can go and figure out what your next move is, make your decision, and then let it go and be present in your life. Don't bring work home to affect your personal life. You need to be able to turn it off. This was tough for me, and I found writing to be a huge relief.

Lists Lighten the Load

I like to list the pros and cons of everything. It helps me get them out of my brain by putting them on paper. By putting my thoughts down on paper, I'm able to see things as they really are.

Defining Success

In order to achieve success, you have to know what it is. Often, you hear people say success is money, fame, a new Bentley, or all these other things. Then, when they get what they thought was success, they're lost. They find that what they were chasing wasn't real success for them.

So What Is Real Success?

It's different for everybody. What success is to me might not be success to somebody else, and what you think success is might not mean success to me. For me, success is leaving a legacy. I want an empire. I want to make a difference. No longer having to introduce myself to people, because they'll already know who I am, is success to me. Think about what success is to you, and then make a one-year plan broken down by quarters to make it happen.

Smartt Steps

1. Before you respond to a situation or make a commitment, ask yourself, "Do I know what my core values really are?" Don't guess them. Write them down. In ink. Your core values should never change. If they do, you're on the wrong track. To live by your core values, you need to take some time to figure out what they are.

2. Explain yourself to yourself in one simple sentence. Here's mine: "Dedicated and driven, I am a creative person with a fire in my belly."

"Great things in business are never done by one person.
They're done by a team of people."
STEVE JOBS

STEP TEN

Collaborate, Collaborate, Collaborate

I learned the importance of positive collaboration when I was out on my own and between jobs. A friend of mine at *The Business Journal* told me the owners of Star Staffing were very interested in meeting with me.

It was nice to be sought out, but knowing they wanted a sales representative (something I had no interest in being), I could have politely declined the meeting. I had a vision of what I thought would lead to a fast-growing and sustainable company, and since Star didn't seem to fit into that vision, why would I "waste time" in this way? At the very least, I knew it would provide a beneficial networking opportunity, so I decided to go to the meeting. The owners of Star met with me and, sure enough, they wanted me to become their sales representative. I was transparent with them about wanting to start my own company, my vision, and my strengths. They listened and asked to meet again. At the second meeting, they informed me that one of the owners had terminal cancer and was phasing herself out of the business. She had handled all the client relations and sales. They wanted me on their team and understood that would require making me a partner in the business. So I told them I would join the company as a sales representative, with the understanding that once I had brought in a certain amount of revenue, I would get my share of ownership. They agreed, and the deal was done. I started at Star Staffing in August 2009, and in three short months, during the recession, I secured the sales number we had agreed upon. Dealing with the attorneys took much longer than I had anticipated, but I was officially an owner by October 2010. Collaboration was key for me, as my strengths were in marketing, public relations, operations, and sales/client relations. My business partner's strengths are in complementary areas: finance, risk management, and processes. Together, we were able to create a dynamic duo and pay tribute to the passing president—who died in December 2010—letting her legacy live on.

Top Ten Reasons to Collaborate

1. You can offer something you can't provide alone.

2. You can learn new things.

3. You can meet new people and learn about them.

4. Collaboration can lead to new opportunities.

5. You can benefit from the lessons learned by a colleague.

6. You can find a solution to a problem you've been grappling with.

7. Collaboration gives you an opportunity to help someone else.

8. You can improve your listening skills.

9. Collaboration provides a good way to demonstrate your leadership skills.

10. Collaboration saves time.

Power of Collaboration

There is a great deal of power in collaboration. I would not be where I am today without the help of my coworkers. Today's fast-paced marketplace requires mutually beneficial partnerships to leverage creativity, experience, and resources with right- and left-brain thinkers who can help you arrive at a solution in less time. When I was a sales representative, I depended on recruiters to find the right talent for employers. Without the recruiting skills they contributed, I wouldn't have succeeded. We all brought strengths to the table. They were constantly recruiting and finding great candidates, and I was constantly selling and building relationships to bring more job orders in. Wherever your collaborations happen—on the boards of organizations or on work teams—you will often need to depend on others to achieve your shared goals.

Set Limits!

Collaboration isn't about being the best of friends but rather about bringing the best you can to the table and partnering for the bigger goal. Think of it as a "talent multiplier."

Partner with People Smarter than You

I've seen this time and time again: the most successful people hire, partner, and surround themselves with people who are smarter than they are. Much as it doesn't make sense to ask fish to climb trees, it makes no sense to expect the impossible of yourself or others. Collaborate with them. Learn from them. Prosper.

Delegate

There are probably people on your team who are great at some of the tasks you're facing every day. Find these people and learn how to share the work. Don't be afraid to let go of things. Biting off more than you can chew can be detrimental to the work's quality, to your sense of well-being, and, ultimately, to your company's success. My to-do list grows and grows, endlessly. I have to delegate. I ask myself who else can do a certain task. If there is no one, then I know I need to do the job myself. If you're saying to yourself, "I'm not an owner yet; I can't delegate," discover opportunities to build that skill set. Offer to chair a committee at work or at your favorite nonprofit and you'll soon learn the fine art of delegating!

Be Honest with Yourself about How You Work Best

In a collaborative work environment, it's important to be absolutely honest about how you work best. In total silence? All right. We can adapt to that. With others, do you work best by actively discussing, diagramming, and making great use of a white board? Perfect. Being honest about how you work best is essential to good team creation and management, and excellent for splitting up goals and tasks between people who have different strengths.

Listen to How Others Work Best

This might seem like a no-brainer, but it's just as important to know how your coworkers work best. If they are easily derailed by interruptions, for instance, your team can make sure those individuals have uninterrupted work time, especially during crunch times or parts of big projects. Agree to give those who are derailed by interruptions three-hour chunks of time, twice a day, when they are not expected to answer calls unless there is an emergency, and save your questions, e-mails, or intranet chatter for times when they can be interrupted—as scheduled.

Keep Others Accountable

Collaborative working environments are great for accountability. When you split up the workload to move a big task forward, you and your team will depend on each other to deliver expected material within the agreed-upon time frame. Setbacks happen, so plan for them. Good planning will help you understand what, across your team, will be affected by setbacks, and you can adjust your timeline as necessary.

Maintaining accountability is true for you, too: be *accountable* to your *team*. If a process isn't working for you, talk about it, and see what kinds of solutions you can come up with. There's definitely a learning curve, especially with a new team, so expect things to change (at least a little bit).

Provide Constant Feedback

Feedback doesn't have to be negative! If a teammate delivers a solid report that's easy to read and digest and full of useful information, give that person props for it. If a couple of people on your team get together and absolutely nail a presentation, celebrate them. When things aren't going so well, express where you think the trouble is but, as I've emphasized before, avoid blame. Collaborative environments are dynamic, and often an improved process will alleviate tension more effectively than scolding a team member.

Know Where You Stand

Understanding the relationship between you and those around you is essential to effective collaboration. I've found that to get a full picture of how I can collaborate effectively with a colleague, I need to have an understanding of my own stress level, overall workload, how supported I feel, and what tools I would need to remove all potential roadblocks. After I have an understanding of where I am, I know how to benchmark team milestones, to make sure we're moving along well. If there is a universal complaint about how often we're interrupted by alerts, for instance, I know where to improve our system.

Be Awake to New Possibilities

Every meeting, every lunch, every hour contains the possibility of collaboration. I believe in collaboration with *everyone*, from the recruiters to my business partner. From the start, I've seen how effective it can be to collaborate with people at all levels of my team because, let's face it, everyone has a valuable perspective. If I'm in a collaborative position with my whole team, I can vet ideas, solve problems, help people feel supported, and be more informed at every turn.

I learned to work well with others through lots of trial and error but also through much input from mentors, bosses, self-help books, and asking questions of my team. I learned to set standards and plainly state my intentions. I ask my team how they like to work together, and then I let them know how I work best. We are as transparent, from top to bottom, as we can possibly be.

We also allow only friendly competition. We're our own best competition, and we use each other's successes as motivation, not as artillery against each other.

I am always open to suggestions. I want to hear what our whole team thinks would make us better, as a team, internally, and for our customers.

Three Ways to Thrive in a Collaborative Environment

1. **Be open to questions, and ask questions yourself.** Brainstorm without judgment, and let ideas grow enough to be able to see them through to their outcomes. Remember, just because nobody's done something a certain way before doesn't mean it's not a good idea. Give your own ideas a chance too!

2. **Leverage personality strengths.** To truly achieve a collaborative environment, you must find the right balance for each person and the group, which can be a process, but it's worth it. Playing to strengths helps everyone feel good about what they're doing and even better about the final product.

3. **Be genuinely supportive, and let your team support you too.** Hear out frustrations; let team members talk through conundrums and leverage what each does best. Even in times of trial, you'll feel cohesive, capable, and unified.

It Takes Collaboration to Make a Difference

Without the support and collaboration of many people, including friends, family, colleagues, mentors, and my business partner, I wouldn't be where I am today. Everyone who has come into my life has made a lasting impact. Whether it was a good or bad impact,

I used it to motivate me to be better than yesterday. When you realize that you—yes, *you*—have the power to be whatever you want to be, things will start changing for you. You are not defined by your past or by your upbringing. You have the power to change that. Break the barriers high, and be the best you that you can be. The only person you should be competing against is yourself.

Smartt Steps

To thrive in a collaborative environment, you need to be able to have honest conversations. Here are three steps to easing a difficult conversation:

1.   Time it right. Figure out the best time and place for the conversation. Over lunch? Over the phone? Via e-mail? What will your schedules and personalities allow?

2.   Be honest and open, and don't be afraid of confrontation. That's the whole point of the conversation, after all. The trick is not to be antagonistic. Don't make it about character; don't start sentences with "You always" or "You never." Instead, stick to the specific problem.

3.   Have a game plan before the conversation begins. How does this person think? Are there any misunderstandings that need to be cleared up? Most of all, know the answer to this question: What is the best outcome of this conversation?

CONCLUSION

Putting on My Shades

The future is bright. It's been a constant learning process, but it's been worth it. Nothing beats hard work, but once you reach that milestone marked "success," don't get complacent. Celebrate, rejoice, and then create new milestones. Aim for higher goals.

My mission is to continue to share practical tips that took me to where I am today. I want to inspire and help people reach new career heights. If I made it here, so can you. Just put these steps into action and deliver on them consistently.

Contact me!

 Nicole@NicoleSmartt.com

 www.Twitter.com/Nicole_Smartt

 www.LinkedIn.com/in/nicolesmartt

 www.Facebook.com/NicoleSmarttBiz

 www.NicoleSmartt.com

NOTES

_____

_____

_____

_____

_____

_____

_____

_____

_____

_____

_____

_____

_____

_____

_____

_____

_____

_____

_____

_____

_____

_____

_____

_____

_____

_____

_____

_____

_____

_____

_____

_____

_____

_____

_____

_____

_____

_____

_____

_____

_____

_____

_____

_____

_____

_____

_____

_____

_____

_____

_____

_____

_____

_____

_____

_____

_____

_____

_____

_____

_____

_____

_____

_____

_____

_____

_____

_____

_____

_____

_____

_____

_____

_____

_____

_____

_____

_____

_____

_____

_____

_____

CPSIA information can be obtained
at www.ICGtesting.com
Printed in the USA
FSOW02n1730250716
23101FS